Can
Catholic Schools
Survive?

All too soon the present day with its dreams and plans becomes part of the past. Not always are the dreams fulfilled and the plans realized. This does not mean that we cease to dream and refuse to plan. [We] built on a dream which had its roots in Faith. When dreams fail because of rushing time, we renew our Faith and point to things Eternal. A greater future will come from the same Faith that built the past.

—T. M. Hesburgh
President
University of Notre Dame

Can
Catholic Schools
Survive?

William E. Brown
Andrew M. Greeley

Sheed and Ward, New York

© Sheed & Ward, Inc., 1970

Library of Congress Catalog Card Number: 70-125828

Standard Book Number: 8362-1079-4

Manufactured in the United States of America

Contents

VI CONTENTS

D. Illustration of Extra Burden and Extra Cost of
Maintaining Catholic Schools at Present Costs   206

E. Sources of Federal Individual Income Taxes   208

F. Average Deductions Claimed in 1966 Federal
Individual Income Tax Returns

Preface

IN THE APPLICATION OF PRINCIPLES, HONEST DIF-
FERENCES OF OPINION CAN ARISE AMONG INTEL-
LIGENT AND SINCERE PEOPLE. WHEN THIS HAPPENS,
ALL SHOULD TAKE CARE TO KEEP ALIVE MUTUAL
ESTEEM AND RESPECT AND STRIVE TO FIND POINTS
OF AGREEMENT FOR EFFICACIOUS AND SUITABLE
ACTION. MEN SHOULD NOT EXHAUST THEMSELVES
IN ENDLESS DISCUSSIONS AND, UNDER THE PRETEXT
OF STRIVING FOR THE BETTER OR THE BEST, FAIL
TO DO THE GOOD THAT IS POSSIBLE AND HENCE
SHOULD BE DONE.

—POPE JOHN XXIII,
Mater et Magistra, para. 238.

The purpose of this book is to impel the Catholic community to do the good that can and should be done now about the crisis in Catholic education. We are presently bogged in not wholly estimable and respectful discussion. The chief action we seem capable of conceiving—though not yet seriously completing—is more research into this and further study of that. Meanwhile, organized Catholic education is dying.

This book does not suggest that discussion end. On the contrary, if Catholic education is not continually and critically discussed, it will eventually die. But in this moment of crisis, if action to resolve the crisis is deferred pending endless discussion of what is better or best, Catholic education will die before our very eyes.

vii

Many people in high places, not only among the intellectuals who write and speak within the Church, but also among teachers and administrators within the Catholic school system, and even among the hierarchy, state or imply that Catholic education via parochial schools and Catholic high schools and colleges should die. "Phased out" is the fashionable term currently in use among those who do not wish to seem intolerant toward tradition-bound conservatives.

This book will address itself chiefly to the question whether the need for the schools has passed. The answer (the book is not a mystery thriller) is that they are needed now more than before. The greater portion of the book will be devoted to showing that, despite serious problems not foreseen even as recently as five years ago, the schools can be sustained and improved to meet today's and tomorrow's educational requirements. Hopefully, the how as well as the why of doing this will reflect Vatican II insights and implications.

While emphasis will be placed on the grade and high schools, other fields and programs of educating Catholics, not least through parish and diocesan councils, will be treated, and conscious effort will be made to suggest priorities and relationships among them. It will be recognized that the getting of Catholic learning, like all education, is a lifetime endeavor of the individual. But we will stress that the giving of education, formally or otherwise, should be a community affair. There it is beset with problems of balance and effectiveness among people-oriented programs, and problems of obtaining and marshalling resources. We will attempt to treat these problems fairly and practically, and our conclusion is that the Catholic community has the required capabilities and resources to solve the problems.

But here and now there is great uncertainty whether the Catholic community has the will to take the difficult steps that will be required. We may have to look hard at ourselves as Christians. Hopefully, we will recommit ourselves to the faith and the Lord's mandate to preach and teach it to all people. After thoughtfully and prayerfully considering how best this may be done for all the people we can reach, we will, again hopefully, conclude that a truly Christian approach to resolving the crisis in Catholic education is impractical and visionary until the alternatives are considered.

A short explanation of the title of Part II may be in order. "Catholic" in my view is as broad as "catholic" in religious matters and hence as broad as "Christian." Not yet? Well, we are what we are, people called "Catholics," and it is as Catholics that we maintain schools to preach and teach a body of views about God and man and the universe called "Catholicism." Changing the names will not change the realities behind the names. It is up to us to change those realities so that "Catholic" and "Catholicism" will, in the eyes and minds of all, recover the connotation of authentic Christian and authentic Christianity. It is precisely the program and process of Catholic education that we must update, in line with Vatican II in order to move from "Catholic" to "Christian" and become truly Catholic.

My wife and I stand, windblown, within the third quartile of the four present generations of Catholics. My mother is still living. Fifteen grandchildren are starting through the Catholic schools. Two children are teaching in the schools as members of one of the great teaching orders of Sisters. My son and his wife teach in a university oriented toward the needs of black students. A son-in-law teaches CCD courses. Despite this rather heavy involvement with progeny and schools, my appeal is to the entire Catholic community, not just to parents of school children, and my plea is in behalf of all programs of education, not just the schools. For I am convinced that there will be no Catholic schools or any other effective programs of Catholic education to support unless Catholic education becomes a community venture, understood and supported by all members of all of the now generations.

I am not a scholar, and my portion of this book is not a scholarly work. It is a work by a lawyer who has had some practical management experience and whose chief experience with education has been as a student, an observer, a reader, an associate of educators. No apology for being a mere lawyer is intended. An eminent judge of a federal court once wrote that the modern lawyer advises his client not only what is permissible but also what is desirable. He is more than a predictor of legal consequences, and his duty to society as well as to his client involves many relevant social, economic, political and philosophical considerations. This lawyer knows that law is not only educational in matters of right and wrong, justice and injustice, but that it can also be creative, particularly with respect to institutions and structures needed by society to achieve its ends and designed to develop each individual as a person who is qualified and motivated to contribute to the common good and entitled to participate in its benefits.

As to my management experience, it would not be surprising to learn in the hereafter that the Holy Spirit is as active in the bureaucracies of big business, big labor and big government as he is in those of the Church. "Participative management," for instance, which has been tested and found to work by many of the largest corporations, is so strikingly like "co-responsibility" in the Church as to lend plausibility to the theory that the basic concept had the same Author. The coincidence might be an example to show how the integration of all fields and sources of knowledge leads to wisdom.

Throughout this book I will draw upon the creative aspects of the law and the insights of modern management. The book will advocate action, and it is inspired by deep concern and not a little anger. It is a synthesis of ideas gathered from sources which would be hard to identify and impossible to footnote. I believe it will reflect the present state of development of the relevant issues and problems and will justify the solutions suggested.

What if some important problem is missed, some proposal is weak or wild? It will not be one man's views which will constitute the blueprint for action with respect to Catholic education. At this point, and perhaps at no point, should there be blueprints. There should be only outline drawings. What we do about Catholic education will be a shifting consensus mysteriously, untraceably and continuously developing out of a process of action. It will not develop from quixotic thrusts of well-intentioned individuals mounting their particular hobby horses. It will develop from organized and concerted action within a structure and through a system for finding out and guiding the doing of what works and discarding what fails.

The book will present a program of action with practical do-it-yourself suggestions. The details may not be complete enough for some persons, not clear enough for others, not suited to the style of still others. It will serve its purpose if the best of it, along with other ideas generated and gathered from who knows where, become part of the background of the people who act. It will serve its purpose if it encourages those people to act by helping to persuade them that Catholic education, especially through the schools, is still worth great effort and sacrifice and can be achieved.

"The people who act". . . Who will they be? The book will indicate plainly enough who they should be. Let it be said here only that the writer is addressing an audience representative of the entire people of God. Among them he sees bishops, priests, sisters, brothers, lay teachers, school administrators, business and professional men and women, white collar workers, blue collar workers, inner city people, suburbanites, parents with children in parochial schools, parents with children in public schools, young marrieds, and young unmarried men and women. There's a piece of the action for all, and it's high time we all move into it.

The writer is tremendously complimented—and complemented— to have Andrew M. Greeley as a collaborator. Father Greeley is a well known sociologist, a teacher of the sociology of education at the University of Chicago, and the Program Director for Higher Education of the National Opinion Research Center. In the latter capacity he collaborated with Philip Rossi in the Greeley-Rossi project of research into the results of Catholic education via the grade and high schools. His opening section, "A Theology of Catholic Education in the 1970's," undergirds everything suggested in my part of this book. If any casual remark or specific suggestions made by this writer is out of line with Father Greeley's development of the concept of the Church as the leader of men's progress in love toward unity and toward the perfection of their God-created and God-assisted natural and spiritual capabilities, write it off as inadvertence or ignorance and make your own applications. The implementation of that concept is the fundamental raison d'être of Catholic education.

One final apologia. The book may sound to many like too much of a preachment and by a layman, at that, who was not ordained to preach. The strictures concerning bishops, for instance, may seem strident and uncharitable. The only justification I can offer is that the need for Catholic education and the possibility of providing it is not being presented by others. The bishops, especially, ought to be talking about it. It must be said and said strongly. I hope that my humility in undertaking the task equals the deep humility of the ordained minister of the Gospel who Sunday after Sunday stands before his congregation to preach virtues which he knows with terror he has obviously not perfected. That man must preach in the hope that the Christians facing him realize that, with St. Paul, he is silently imploring them to pray to God in his behalf that while preaching to others he himself does not become a castaway.

To perform the hard tasks of authentic Christians we must love each other authentically and support each other unitedly. To lead effectively the bishops must lead as a group, and they must be followed by other Christians as a community. Our responsibilities are diverse, but they must be shared equally. Our task will be greatly eased if we go about it with humor—that great sign of understanding that, despite the seriousness of our tasks and the difficulties of performing them, we are still children who were created to play before God and to delight in playing with our fellowmen.

It will be immediately noted that this book pays little attention to the past. The history of institutions is important insofar as it is used to help explain the institutions. Too often, however, history is examined and reexamined because it is felt that we are somehow determined by it, that we are such and such because of our history, and that there is nothing we can do except follow a projection of it. Hence, if we study history and extrapolate it carefully, we will see our future. The point of view of this book is that it is the present, the existential situation, that contains more than the past does of the needs, the promise and the hope for the future of Catholic education.

At any rate, many scholarly works have been written covering the history of Catholic education, and they are readily available to anyone interested in that method of arriving at an explanation of the present situation. No doubt history does contain many helpful facts, just as genes and chromosomes inherited from some ancestor help explain ourselves to ourselves and others if we could only identify them and confidently ascertain the effects of their mixture. But morbid preoccupation with genes and chromosomes is a currently fashionable waste of time and emotional energy for most of us compared with shaping up in line with what we jolly well know, or what our neighbors tell us, is wrong with us. So, too, it is more profitable to spend our time and emotional energy tackling the very obvious things we can see, or the world tells us, are wrong with Catholic education. We should look for remedies in the known present and not for excuses in the ambiguous past.

This writer's portion of this book represents his effort to update his own thinking. The book treats problems not perceived when he was on the Holy Name Society Speakers' Bureau some years ago: the need to rethink and resell the purpose of Catholic education, especially education by means of the schools, the need to renew and broaden the content of that education and find better methods of presenting it, to cope with unforeseen new costs, and to pull the loose administrative ends together into a system.

Many particular solutions suggested in this book may be outdated tomorrow. But its basic suggestion will never be outdated. It is that we should develop a frame of mind and devise a structure geared to adaptation so that never again will the Catholic community be caught twenty years, or even two years behind the times in pursuing its mandated purpose of teaching and witnessing the word of God to all nations.

How to do this is one thing. Why do it is another. The why should be answered first with deep understanding and strong conviction, or the how will be found too difficult to be considered worthwhile.

Milwaukee, Wisconsin   William E. Brown
August 15, 1970

Part 1.

A Theology of Catholic Education in the 1970's

Andrew M. Greeley

PROGRAM DIRECTOR,
NATIONAL OPINION RESEARCH CENTER
UNIVERSITY OF CHICAGO

Introduction

It is the purpose of this section to attempt to state a positive theology of Catholic education. I use "education" in the narrow sense of the word, equating it with schools. There has been a tendency in some Catholic circles recently to expand the term, "Catholic education," to include any instructional activity in which the Church engages. There may be value in this use of the term, but in the present essay I am limiting my comments strictly to Catholic schools.

Since the very beginning of their existence in this country, Catholic schools have been a subject of controversy both inside and outside the Church. As Robert Dougherty Cross makes clear in his book, *The Emergence of Liberal Catholicism in America,** the controversy over whether Catholics should close their schools is not a phenomenon of the 1960's. Quite the contrary, it developed before the beginning of the present century.

Inside the Catholic community the two principal issues being discussed seem to be: Are Catholic schools possible? If they are possible, should they exist?

While both issues have considerable theoretical interest and can present challenges to wit and ingenuity at liberal Catholic cocktail parties, they are both ultimately unresolved and irrelevant. Catholic schools do exist. They are not going to be eliminated, if only because the pressures on the public school systems in the large metropolitan centers in the northeast and north central sections of the country make such elimination inconceivable.

* Cambridge, Mass.: Harvard Univ. Press, 1958.

But, if one concedes that Catholic schools will continue but that they are not absolutely necessary for the protection of the faith of Catholic students, then one is faced with relevant and practical questions. What are the schools for? What unique contribution can they make to the rest of American education?

It is a sign of the intellectual bankruptcy of American Catholicism that these questions have not been asked. In these pages we will attempt to explain why the world's largest Catholic school system has been incapable of articulating a philosophy or theology which would give it direction and purpose and of raising the question of whether it may be possible to develop such a theology.

As far as the author knows, almost no American Catholic theologian is attempting to find a set of goals and values for Catholic oriented education. Perhaps theologians are afraid that, if they do research this question, they will be accused of "defending" Catholic education, and there is nothing more unpopular in American Catholicism today than "defending" Catholic schools. Yet the theologians who seem so interested in using the data of human experience as a basis for their theological reflections have overlooked the extraordinary experience of the Catholic school system in the United States. They are content, it would seem, with dismissing it with a few well-chosen clichés selected from the appropriate liberal journals. The school system has educated millions of people, numbers thousands of institutions, and it has tens of thousands of personnel. It has been created by the voluntary offerings of what was until very recently an impoverished segment of the population of the United States. But it is apparently a phenomenon which the theorists of American Catholicism did not deem worthy of serious reflection. They conclude, rather, that the phenomenon is going to go away.

The conclusion frees them from any concern about elaborating theoretical perspectives from which to consider Catholic schools in the United States. There is no point in speculating about something that is going to go out of existence, especially when such speculations classify you as a defender of Catholic schools, or even worse, as a conservative. But if the romantic assumption that the Catholic schools are going to vanish is wrong, then those theorists who refuse to elaborate a theology of Catholic education are, to put the matter charitably, negligent.

We believe that Catholic schools in some form or other are going to survive for the indefinite future. They may decline in enrollment; they may encounter severe crises of finance and personnel, though in this latter respect they are no different from American public schools, but they will continue to exist.

This section, then, is not new and it is not an attempt to defend Catholic schools. It is based on the assumption that they will continue to exist and that a theoretical perspective about their goals would help to orient the schools to the challenges they ought to be facing. I turn my attention to these questions not because I am particularly qualified as a philosopher or theologian, but because those who are so qualified do not seem to be interested in the subject. Furthermore, I am appalled at the low state of morale of Catholic educators, a condition which is not based on any empirical evidence of either declining support in the Catholic population or declining academic effectiveness. Much of the morale problem may be caused by theoretical uncertainties. Catholic educators are asking themselves two questions: Should our schools exist? What makes them different from other schools?

The pertinent questions, however, are, it seems to me: What should we be doing and what unique contributions can we make? The purpose of the present section is to provide some tentative answers to both questions.

Some will argue that the author is biased in favor of Catholic schools. One of the peculiar rules of the present debate is that anyone who does not advocate the immediate abolition of all Catholic schools is said to be biased in favor of them, although those who criticize Catholic schools are assumed to be completely free of bias.

My own interests in Catholic education are rooted in some nine years of empirical research on Catholic schools, none of which was financed by the Church. I am not on the staff of any Catholic school and never have been. I am not part of Catholic education administration and never have been. None of my research projects has ever been financed by the Catholic educational system. I have never acted as a consultant to any diocese or school administration. At one time I responded to an invitation and volunteered to serve on the Catholic school board of my own archdiocese, only to be told in a form letter that others more qualified than I had been chosen for the board. It is very unlikely that I will ever have anything to do with Catholic schools for the rest of my life. It is embarrassing to have to take such a "loyalty oath." Anyone attempting to say something constructive about future projections for Catholic education is immediately suspect. When the writer is a priest, he is even more suspect. But my interest in the future development of Catholic education is based on the sociological insight that the Catholic schools will continue, the educational insight that they have an important contribution to make in the rest of American education and the theological insight that Catholic schools can play an important part in the mission of the Church.

1. The Educational Experience

Pompous language and empty generalities seem to correlate negatively with skill and competence. Formal education is a human activity which has a good deal of the former and precious little of the latter. Even though the human race has engaged in one kind of formal education or another for several millennia, it has made relatively little progress in understanding what the educational process involves. The basic instructional method (teacher in the classroom) has not progressed very much since the Bronze Age, and the fads and fashions that sweep across the educational realm promise dramatic change but produce very little practical impact. Young people are educated not because of what their teachers do but despite what their teachers do. The educational enterprise is about as sophisticated as was medicine when the principal therapeutic technique was bloodletting.

But the practice of medicine is easy compared to the practice of education. The human body is a complex intricate mechanism, but it is simplicity itself compared to the human mind. Medical doctors are more skillful at their work than teachers only in part because they are superior in intelligence and paid better. Doctors are more successful than teachers simply because doctors' tasks are much easier than the tasks of teachers.

The general failure to educate is not the result of the lack of goodwill, but rather the result of the immense complexities and difficulties involved in the educational enterprise. Knowing what we do now about the failures of the educational fads of the past, we can perhaps be more moderate in our expectations of notable

7

educational successes in the immediate future. Nevertheless, it does seem likely that our increased sophistication about the human personality and the way it evolves and grows can in remaining decades of the century lead to very substantial progress in education. Therefore, we begin with the assumption that even though education is still in a primitive stage of development, it may well be on the brink of considerable progress.

There are four basic goals in the educational enterprise: training in basic skills of cognition and expression, transmission of the values of a cultural heritage, development of critical intelligence and training scholars to explore beyond the frontiers of our present knowledge. In the division of labor that marks the educational enterprise, the first goal is emphasized in the primary school, the second goal on the secondary level, the third in higher education and the fourth in graduate schools. But the division of labor is by no means exclusive. Critical intelligence, for example, does not suddenly emerge when the student matriculates as a college freshman. The ability to consider alternatives intelligently and to communicate towards consensus presumes that the student has mastered the mechanical skills of reading and writing, but many certainly have not. The student should also have at least an inchoate system of values which provides him with a personality core strong enough to support him in his consideration of alternatives and his dialog towards consensus. Finally, that curiosity which is necessary for the scholar begins to develop, not on the day he takes the graduate record exam, but when he first sets foot in his kindergarten classroom.

For most of the history of the Western world, it was assumed that all education except the most elementary was the prerogative of the privileged few. Aristotle's free man, the English upper-class gentleman, the continental aristocrat, were to be educated, or at least the male members of such social classes had the right to education. For the rest of society, education was deemed unnecessary, probably useless and possibly dangerous. The United States, however, decided very early in its career as a nation that every man was a free man, every man an aristocrat, every man a gentleman and, therefore, every man had a right to an education. At first, grammar school education was considered to be every man's privilege. Then, a high school diploma was viewed as part of the heritage of every American. Finally, in the closing years of the century, Americans argued that everyone has the right to attend college. Some say, not altogether facetiously, that a doctoral degree will soon be considered the prerogative of every citizen.

It is easy to satirize the American faith in education for every man, but one should not forget that the belief is a noble and impressive one. It is rooted in a conviction about the dignity, integrity and value of the individual and does great credit to the society which has committed itself to such a conviction. But society may deserve somewhat less credit for the intelligence and sophistication with which it has pursued the goal. However, I would like to point out that the typical black American is more likely to attend college than is the typical citizen of West Germany. It is certainly not my intention to argue that the lot of the black American is better than that of the West German. I only wish to show that despite our obvious social and economic deficiencies, the United States still has a commitment to universal education that is matched nowhere in the world.

Unfortunately, this noble commitment has not always been supported by either intelligent planning or intelligent allocation of resources. We have built marvelous buildings in which to house our students, but we give our teachers salaries and social status that will guarantee that the most intelligent and able young people will choose occupations other than primary and secondary education. We give the college professors more status than his colleagues at the lower education levels, but we compensate for that by awarding the highest prestige to those faculty members who spend the smallest amount of time with students and the greatest amount of time in activities that have nothing to do with the instruction of students. The American faith in education is limitless; one might almost say it is blind. Part of that faith, apparently, is the assumption that the educational experience works its magic almost automatically. Therefore, one need not give too much concern to either the subtleties of the process of education or the skills of those who are supposed to direct the process. So long as the school buildings are properly lighted, properly heated, properly protected from fire and equipped with the proper washroom facilities, the American taxpayer is not greatly concerned about what happens in the schools, save on those occasions when it is called to his attention that either Communism or sex is being taught in the classroom.

The problem is aggravated by the fact that educators have promised far more than they can deliver. If the American republic has faith in the educability of every man, American educators seem to have faith in their own ability, not merely to educate, but to solve every problem which faces American society.

In the nineteenth century educators were convinced that they could Americanize, civilize and Protestantize the Europeans who were coming to America. For some reason or other, they were puzzled when some of these immigrants organized their own school system. More recently, Dr. James B. Conant has said that the public school, particularly the public secondary school, is the great integrator of American society because all Americans, regardless of race, religion or ethnic background come together there to learn how to be Americans. That integration does not occur is clear at the present time, but it ought to have been clear to anybody who spent much time inside the American secondary school when Conant and his colleagues were arguing that the secondary school would integrate America's pluralistic society.

Finally, we hear today that education is going to solve the problems of the city. Our higher educational institutions, having failed to achieve the goals of liberal education, are now asking us to believe that they should be permitted to descend upon the inner city to eliminate its social problems. Our primary and secondary educators assure us that if we permit them the right racial balances in their schools, they will move towards a solution to the problem of education for the underprivileged, a promise which seems singularly hollow when one realizes that the achievement of American education among the privileged is at best dubious. It is surely a rather strange form of pride, not to say blindness, for an institution which has been none too successful at its own goals to suddenly claim jurisdiction over other goals.

One cannot blame American educators for delivering so little.

The education of immigrants, the creation of a cultural context and the education of the economically disadvantaged are immensely difficult tasks about which relatively little is known. It is not at all surprising that little progress has been made thus far. What is surprising is that educators have had the gall to claim so much, and the continued gall to repeat ever bigger claims despite the fact that they have been so unsuccessful in delivering on previous claims. If the American public expects so much from education, far more in fact than it has any right to expect, the reason is largely that American educators have promised far more than they had any right to promise.

The problems of American educational enterprise are made worse by the incredible bureaucratization that afflicts it. Any complex society is bound to elaborate bureaucratic structures with built-in tendencies toward stagnation and immobility. But for some reason that we must leave to the further research of the psychologists and sociologists who specialize in deviancy and pathology, education has singularly powerful tendencies to stagnation and immobility. The stranglehold of faculty committees over curriculum reform, of trustees over institutional innovation and of administrators and principals over creative teachers is appalling. Not all college presidents and not all school superintendents and administrators are pompous, arrogant and easily threatened men. But one sometimes finds it hard to escape the conclusion that there is a far higher proportion of these qualities among professional educators than there is in other occupations. The root of the problem is that society expects the educational leader to be wise. Therefore, he is constrained on frequent occasions to act and speak as though he were wise. There is nothing wrong with such behavior unless the educator begins to take what he says seriously and to believe that he actually is wise. When that happens he begins his love affair with the sound of his own voice and the institution he is responsible for is in serious trouble.

If American education is in deep trouble—one need only read the daily newspaper to see that it is—it is not difficult to understand the reason. It has made big promises which it should never have made. Then it has failed to fulfill the promises. It has laid claim to a substantial share of the nation's income, but it has not used its money wisely. It has talked about the student and his growth, but it is atrophying in a complex bureaucratic structure in which the student is quickly forgotten. It is frequently presided over by men who, despite their high-flown language, simply do not know what they are doing.

Furthermore, the educational enterprise is an ideal scapegoat that can be blamed for everything that goes wrong. Are young people smashing windows? It's the school's fault. Are other young people driving recklessly or smoking pot? Once again, the schools are to blame. Are some children racist? Why didn't the schools educate their racism out of them? Is my child doing poorly in school? Then it must be the school's fault. Or, is my child emotionally tense and anxious? Surely that couldn't be blamed on his home. Therefore, it must be his teacher's responsibility. Has Communism taken over China? We must have courses on anti-Communism in the schools. Is religion in trouble? It's because nobody is reading the Bible in schools anymore. One almost wonders what would happen in the American society if the schools disappeared and there was no other group to blame for our frustrations and disappointments.

As the twentieth century lurches towards a conclusion, the American educational enterprise is in its most serious crisis. Costs are going up partly because a new generation of teachers is displaying the same kind of militancy that steel workers and packing house workers displayed three and four decades ago. Parents blame the schools for the cultural problems that afflict their children and demand more control over the schools and more change in the educational experience. Restless college and high school students protest against the lack of challenge in their educational experience. State legislators grow more and more suspicious of increases in school operating expenses. Educational administrators, mired in bureaucratic complexity, are overwhelmed by the problems they must face. And an increasing number of thoughtful observers suggest that the only way to respond to the educational problems of the inner city is to set up a series of private school systems which can effectively compete with the immobile public school monopoly.

Within the context of this situation in the American educational enterprise, I want to make the following observations:

Catholic schools are not the only schools in trouble;

Both Catholic and public schools are scapegoats for frustrations and anxiety;

Both Catholic and public schools have financial difficulties;

Both Catholic and public schools have enemies who would like to see them destroyed;

Both Catholic and public schools suffer from unrealistic verbalizing.

The American educational enterprise is not going to go away. It is not going to be reformed overnight. It is not even going to change at all simply because people are angry at it. The best that can be expected at the present time is more modesty from the educators, more patience and realism from the general public and more willingness from both for constant experimentation, reevaluation and innovation. The only hope for growth is the development of a consensus which says, "We really don't know much about education, and that's no one's fault; but the time has come to try to learn more about what education involves and to experiment to improve the process."

In our attempts to understand more about education and to do it better, there are four hopeful propositions upon which we can meditate. None of the ideas is very new, though our increase in sophistication in the social sciences perhaps helps us to see more clearly their implications. I think that whatever educational progress we make in the decades ahead of us will be based on more adequate understanding of the truth of these four propositions.

People Educate Themselves

No one can force another person to learn. We can demand that students write term papers, pass examinations, memorize vast amounts of information and acquire the appropriate grades, but we really can't make them learn. People learn because they want to, because they need to, because they understand that certain kinds of knowledge and skills are important for their lives or because they enjoy it. The best the teacher can do is to facilitate self-education. Two conclusions can be drawn from this observation, one pessimistic, the other optimistic. Pessimists can decide that much of what goes on in schools is an utter waste of time. Students exchange correct answers for desired grades, but this has nothing to do with learning. Optimists say that, despite our poor understanding of the educational process, and despite the nonsense and foolishness in which we so frequently engage in schools, a substantial number of young people are going to be reasonably well-educated. The young learn no matter what we do to them and no matter what we don't do to them. If teachers, administrators and educational bureaucrats could only resign themselves to the fact that they will at best play a relatively small role in the self-education of the individual human person, they might be able to play that role far more effectively.

Human Learning Takes Place in Communities

Or, to put the matter somewhat more bluntly, most young people learn far more from their friends than they do from their teachers. We still do homage to the myth that what we have out there in front of us in the classroom is thirty individuals, but the classroom is really a congeries of groups, subgroups and demigroups. The reality of the interaction network of the members of the classroom is no less powerful because we choose to ignore it. The friendship group controls the productivity of the learning situation, just as the friendship group of workers in the factory controls the productivity of its members. The secret of the educational process, then, is not to try to fight the group because the teacher who does that will quickly find that his power is very minor compared to the power of the group. Instead of fighting the group he should "co-opt" it for educational purposes. But "co-option" is not the proper word because it implies exploitation and also because it's not likely to work. The wise teacher, understanding that learning is going on in and through the group, sees his role as the facilitator of the group learning experience. Such a teacher follows the wisdom of the Irish adage, "If you can't beat them, join them."

Learning Is Personal

The educational experience does not involve merely acquiring certain knowledge and certain skills. It is an integral part of the development of the total human personality. Although the school itself is particularly concerned with the cognitive development of the child, it cannot ignore the development of the rest of his personality, nor the delicate interrelationships between cognitive and noncognitive development.

The college freshman who cannot write a decent paragraph feels personally inadequate because of this deficiency, but the deficiency in its turn is rooted in a sense of inadequacy over his own ideas, an inadequacy which hides behind convolute verbiage. Learning how to write decent English prose involves both cognitive and emotional growth, and the two simply cannot be separated. A person will learn only when he perceives reinforcement for his dignity, integrity and value as a human being. If, however, the educational enterprise casts doubt on his self-esteem or subjects it to testing and approval, then he is not going to learn very much.

As Joseph Spaeth has pointed out, intellectual development at the college level can take place only in circumstances where someone says to the student in effect, "I will listen to what you think." Unfortunately, both challenging and supportive response to students is rare at every educational level.

The teacher cannot, of course, be a psychiatrist, but he must take into account the complex emotional context in which each of his students lives, and he must also be aware of the therapeutic contribution that authentic academic achievement can make. Teachers must be far more psychologically sophisticated than they presently seem to be (and this does not, God help us, mean more courses in educational psychology). A teacher must also be far more sophisticated about his own personality because unless he understands his personal reaction to his students he is likely to be inadequate in the very fluid context in which learning occurs.

Learning Is Relational

It is an experience that not only involves the growth of one person but the interaction, sometimes on a very intimate level, of two persons. There is a great deal of enthusiasm presently about teaching machines, although most teaching machines are simply elaborate forms of the blackboard. Whether the instruments will be intelligently used or not depends on the person who is using them. But there does not seem to be much reason to doubt that through technology part of the learning process can be automated. Certain kinds of skills and information can probably be acquired as readily, if not more readily, from a machine than they can from another human being. Nonetheless, the most efficient teaching machine ever developed has been around for a long time. It is called a book, and we have not yet made effective use of it. On the contrary, given the fear of books inculcated in many upper and middle class children during their education, one can expect that in years to come children will also be afraid of teaching machines.

Whatever the potential effectiveness of teaching machines, old or new, the most important educational experiences still take place in what is essentially a human relationship. It is not a relationship as intimate as marriage or psychotherapy, but ideally speaking, the relationship between teacher and student ought to be more intimate than most other human relationships because it concerns intimately human aspects of the personality: truth, goodness and beauty. Only if friendship and love exist between teacher and student can the relationship be a fully successful one. Love is difficult in any relationship, but it is more difficult when it must cross generational lines because so many of the unresolved conflicts out of the past subtly pervade the relational climate. Teachers and students do not like each other because they fear each other. Fear and love cannot coexist.

Although there is not statistical data to prove it, I believe that the really good teacher is the one who is confident. He is not afraid of his students. Therefore, he can give himself to the teaching relationship. The good student, on the other hand, is a student who has enough confidence in his own validity to realize that a wrong answer or a poor grade does not affect his basic worth. However, the emotional baggage both teacher and student bring to their relationship makes it very difficult for either to display much trust. The teacher knows he is being evaluated by his students, and the student knows he is being evaluated, indeed, being graded for life, by his professor. Small wonder that the relationships are bad. Small wonder that little learning takes place.

Despite the somewhat dismal educational situation at the present time, it seems to me that there are some grounds for hope in these four propositions. If we are willing to view the teacher as someone who facilitates self-education and peer group education, as one who creates a climate in which the total human person can grow, and finally, as one who radiates love and trust in a learning experience, we may make considerable progress in years to come.

The Crisis in Catholic Education

We noted above that there seems to be a negative correlation between pomposity and competence. Those human activities where there is a fair amount of competence and clarity of thought are relatively unafflicted by conventional wisdom. Therefore, one should not be surprised to learn that education abounds in conventional wisdom. Catholic education is no exception.

It is appropriate at the beginning of this section on the present condition of Catholic education to discuss the major tenets of the conventional wisdom about the Catholic schools.

Graduates of Catholic schools are not substantially different religiously from Catholics who went to public schools. Whatever differences exist can be explained by family background and not by the schools.

Catholic schools are "divisive," that is, they isolate Catholics from an "integrated American consensus."

Catholic schools are academically inferior because Catholic classrooms are overcrowded.

Catholic schools are exhausting the resources of the American Church. The money spent and the personnel employed in the schools could be better used on more effective forms of apostolic endeavor.

Catholic schools are a hindrance to the American Church because only a minority of Catholics of school age attend such schools.

Confraternity of Christian Doctrine (CCD), released time, evening or Sunday classes are where the action really is. They are more effective means of training Catholics for the postconciliar era, and they are real apostolic efforts.

Catholic higher education is a wasteful use of resources because of the very high ratio of clergy or religious to students in Catholic colleges and the very low ratio of clergy or religious to students in the Newman apostolate.

American Catholics cannot afford to support their schools.

Catholics are withdrawing support from parochial education.

Graduates of Catholic schools are no less prejudiced than Catholics who went to public schools.

Catholic schools are not serving the poor.

Catholic schools cannot serve both the poor in the inner city and the rich in the suburbs.

There is no academic freedom in Catholic colleges.

Catholic colleges are not popular with their alumni so parents will not send their children to the Catholic colleges which they themselves attended.

These ideas have been repeated so frequently and with such a degree of conviction that they have become sacred and unassailable. Since everyone knows that they are true, they need no evidence to support them, and anyone odd enough to question them is assumed to be either dishonest or a fool.

However, all the above propositions are false.

The graduates of Catholic schools do score higher on measures of religious behavior than do the Catholic graduates of public schools. The difference, far from being explained away by family background, is reinforced when family background is held constant. The difference between Catholic school graduates and public school graduates is most striking among those who come from devout family backgrounds.

Despite intensive efforts by a number of researchers, not the slightest bit of evidence has been uncovered of the alleged "divisive" effect of Catholic schools.

All data available indicates that Catholic schools are on the average somewhat superior academically to public schools. Catholic secondary schools are considerably superior to public high schools. Nor is there any evidence in any research of a relationship between classroom size and the academic performance of students.

It is fallacious to assume that the money going to Catholic

schools would be available for other purposes. Catholic schools are not draining personnel from other apostolates. Catholic school administrators have recruited and trained their own personnel and probably most of the personnel used in other religious institutions.

More than two-thirds of Catholic children whose parents want religious education for them attend Catholic schools. A very large number of children whose parents desire religious education for them are not in Catholic schools because they live in areas where there are no Catholic schools.

There is no empirical evidence to support the contention that CCD is an adequate form of religious instruction, nor is there any theoretical reason to assume that one can do better in one hour a week than one can do in twenty hours a week.

The ratio of Catholic students actually interested in participating in Newman programs to Newman personnel is probably little different than the ratio of students to religious faculty at Catholic colleges. The fallacy which assumes that every Catholic at a non-Catholic college is pounding the door of the Newman club or would respond to any kind of Newman initiative is patently absurd.

While the costs of Catholic education, like that of all other education, have gone up, we do not know enough about the economics of Catholic higher education to say how much it costs. Nor are we able to say with any degree of certainty that the relative costs are greater now than they were in the 1930's. The alleged inability or unwillingness of the Catholic population to pay for Catholic schools has not been demonstrated.

Since the *Catholic Digest* study in 1953, the question of support for Catholic schools has been included in a wide variety of surveys in many parts of the country. The percentage of the Catholic population supporting Catholic schools has not deviated in that period of time. Some 70 percent of the Catholic population has consistently favored continuation of the schools despite all the pressures of the conventional wisdom. Those who say Catholics do not want the schools are using the same argument as those who say that the people cannot afford the schools, and they have not bothered to ask the opinions of the people for whom they presume to be speaking.

Graduates of Catholic schools, and particularly of Catholic colleges, do score lower on measures of racial prejudice than do Catholic graduates of public schools.

The statement that Catholic schools are doing no service to the poor is an insult to the heroic efforts of priests and nuns in the inner cities, and it is contradicted by the overwhelming popularity of Catholic schools with the black citizens of our large cities.

There is no reason to assume, at least until convincing data are adduced, that American Catholics cannot afford to serve both the ghetto and the suburb, both the poor and the affluent, and a large segment of the population somewhere in between. The argument that Catholicism must choose is simply one more example of the fallacy of the "two alternatives." Furthermore, the idea that the financial resources would be available to serve the inner city if suburbanites were rejected from the Catholic school systems would be laughable if it were not so foolish.

At present, only one American Catholic college is on the censure list of the American Association of University Professors, and a number of careful research projects have found no more evidence of abuse of academic freedom in Catholic colleges than in any other kind of college. The argument frequently heard that theological commitment and a disinterested search for truth are incompatible ignores the fact that faculties of most great American universities have their own kind of theoretical commitments that are as rigid and dogmatic as any to be found in the Catholic schools.

Recent research indicates that the alumni of Catholic schools are more pleased with their higher educational experience than the typical American alumni, despite their awareness of the weaknesses of the Catholic colleges. Their greatest satisfaction is based on what is the strongest correlate of satisfaction for all college alumni—the college's contribution to the development of life values. Furthermore, the graduates of Catholic colleges are more likely than typical alumni to send their children to the school they attended.

The gap between the conventional wisdom and reality is, therefore, immense, and yet the conventional wisdom continues to be accepted. Recently I was asked by a colleague at the University of Chicago to speak to a workshop that he supervises each summer for those interested in "nonpublic" education. As one might have expected, most of the participants in the seminar were young priests and religious. I discussed with them not the perennial and hearty controversy over whether there ought to be Catholic schools, but rather my own notions of what healthy directions future development in Catholic schools should take. During the question period, however, my positive suggestions for the future were ignored, and we returned to the conventional wisdom and the conventional discussions. What surprised me was not so much the resurgence of the conventional wisdom as its presence among the young, and what offended me slightly was the sly air of superiority with which the questions were asked. These young people were not interested in constructive directions for the future, nor were they much concerned about facts. They knew what the future was going to be, and they knew what reality was. They were convinced that I was a defender of the status quo, a conservative who was biased in favor of Catholic schools, and probably some sort of crypto agent for the American hierarchy. But what was most disturbing was that they repeated their arguments with the same kind of intelligence and sensitivity that one would expect from fourth graders reciting the multiplication tables from memory. They were parrots squawking a party line, quite incapable of asking any probing questions about the validity of the line. I would almost be tempted to say that they were marvelous proof of the inferiority of the Catholic schools which produced them if the same kind of dedication to other forms of conventionalism was not so typical of most young Americans in our present all too Romanticist era.

So the conventional wisdom lives, but one must still ask why.

Why, if the support of the Catholic population of the schools is undeviating, is the leadership of the schools so completely persuaded that they are in a time of great crisis? Why is enrollment declining, at least in the primary schools? Why is it increasing on the secondary and higher levels? Why are the Catholic educators themselves the most enthusiastic exponents of the conventional wisdom? Why are some bishops and school administrators so pathetically eager to close down or phase out certain Catholic schools? Why, indeed, is this crisis taking place precisely at the time when outside the Church there is more sympathy for and support for Catholic education than ever before? Why does it seem likely that the first government check might arrive the day after the last Catholic bishop has closed down the last Catholic school in his diocese? Why, when working with young people is an extraordinarily attractive career, do Catholic priests and religious seem so eager to get out of their schools? Why, when the overwhelming evidence of empirical research refutes the conventional wisdom, is it still clung to so tenaciously by those who presumably ought to be pleased by the apparent success of their work?

Catholic educators are discouraged, of course, because their work has been moderately successful, but it has not been exceptionally successful. Such discouragement they must share with all educators. Furthermore, Catholic schools are scapegoats just as all schools are scapegoats, and much of the frustration and dissatisfaction with the present situation in the American Church can easily be projected into the schools. Finally, self-hatred is inevitable in the later stages of the acculturation process of any immigrant group. So it is inevitable that the generation of Catholics which made the big leap from the Catholic subcultures to the larger society would feel ashamed of anything specifically Catholic and would be hypercritical of their own origins. But self-hatred, scapegoating and discouragement are hardly adequate by themselves to explain the crisis of confidence in Catholic education.

And a crisis of confidence it certainly is, for the basic problem facing Catholic schools in the United States is not loss of external support, but the internal collapse of morale. There is a loss of nerve, a loss of conviction, a loss of faith, a loss of enthusiasm. This is the root of the problem of Catholic education. If such an elaborate and imposing edifice could be tipped over by a handful of armchair critics completely unencumbered by empirical data, then something seriously must have happened inside the edifice. But what was it?

The answer is reasonably simple. Catholic schools, like the rest of the American Church, have been caught in the currents and countercurrents stirred up by the intersection of two transitions, from Counter-Reformation to Ecumenical Age, and from immigrant slum to professional suburbs.

Until 1960 the American Church existed in the world of the firm, rigid, immutable certainties of the Counter-Reformation, and it built a broad, systematic defense against the threats of a hostile non-Catholic society. It was determined to protect the faith of the immigrants against all onslaughts. The scientific revolution, modern culture and non-Catholic churches were dangers to be avoided. And in the state of siege, dialog with the enemy or discussion with one's leaders was out of the question. A state of war existed, and iron discipline was required to win the war. But the defensive, protectionist style of the immigrant church was irrelevant by 1960 because the overwhelming number of American Catholics were no longer immigrants, and Catholics under forty were as likely to be college graduates and economically and socially successful as were their Protestant counterparts. Even though the style and attitude of the parish diocese was still essentially protectionist, there was nothing much left that had to be protected.

Similarly, the upheaval of the Vatican Council demolished the rigid certainties of the Counter-Reformation and called into question attitudes and values which previously had been beyond question in the Catholic Church. If the meat on Friday rule could be changed, if Mass could be said in English, if a papal commission could be convened to study the birth control issue, then the whole tightly connected and supposedly immutable value system was open to serious question. It was all well and good to say that the substance of doctrine could not be changed, but it was no longer clear where the distinction between substance and accident could be drawn.

In another work* I have described in some detail how the three institutions—hierarchy, clergy and intellectuals—which could have been expected to provide leadership through the crisis of double transition failed to respond to the challenges. In this particular section, I will comment only on the ways in which these three institutions failed to cope with the crisis in Catholic education.

With some very notable exceptions, the American hierarchy was chosen because it was "safe," that is, docile and timid. Although the bishops of the country are for the most part honest and sincere

---

* *Religion in the Year 2000* (New York: Sheed & Ward, Inc., 1969).

men, and although many of them have demonstrated far more openness to change than most priests or laity of their own generation, only a few of them can be described as charismatic and imaginative leaders. But if some sense of direction is to be maintained in a time of chaos and confusion, charismatic and creative leaders are required. The hierarchy has responded to the crisis in Catholic schools in two predictable fashions:

1. They have denounced the enemies of Catholic education for daring to assume that anything at all was missing in the traditional conduct of Catholic schools. They confidently asserted that there was no possibility of change in Church policy on education.

2. Whenever the financial going got even a little bit difficult, many bishops promptly closed their schools.

They were not then able to steer a middle course between no change and abandoning schools, and the dramatic move from one position to another easily persuaded some Catholic educators that the resolute pronouncements about sustaining Catholic schools were simply ways of whistling in the dark.

The same bishop who publicly announces that the closing of Catholic schools is unthinkable will privately concede that he doesn't see how his people can possibly afford to continue to support the schools. His problem is not hypocrisy, but lack of imagination. He is not willing to contemplate change in the administration, financing or goals of Catholic education, and he is not willing to take any risks to develop new means of financing. He even refuses to do serious research to see if his assumptions about dismal prospects in the future are valid. We must either maintain the old system pretty much as it is, or we must abandon it completely.

A more serious problem is to be found in the clergy and religious staff of Catholic schools. Most of them, we fear, were recruited as adolescents and trained in such a way as to persist in many adolescent behavior patterns. Our superiors treated us like adolescents, both in the training period and in our work in later life precisely because the passive, immature, dependent person was most easily controlled. Unfortunately, the passive, dependent person never learns to exercise initiative or responsibility and never acquires very deep internalized convictions or commitments. Perhaps convictions and commitments were not required in the Counter-Reformation in the Church. But then that marvelous old Italian gentleman threw open his window and the hurricane came in which knocked down the props. Now many priests and religious must act as if they were mature adults capable of self-actualization, initiative and responsibility. Under such circumstances what is astonishing is not that so many regress to adolescent behavioral patterns, but that so many do not.

Not only is this kind of priest and religious incapable of coping with the complexity and fluidity of a time of transition, but he is also most reluctant to engage in any systematic effort to acquire new convictions or deepen and strengthen those he already has. The Catholic schools are in crisis and confusion. The immature priest or religious caught in the midst of this confusion discovers that he is not sure what he is doing or why he is doing it, and he loses his nerve. But if losing one's nerve is an unpleasant experience, running the risk of thinking through convictions so that one may reacquire one's nerve is even more unpleasant. Better to accept disaster all around and then flee from the sea of disaster than to engage in delicate, subtle and courageous activity to determine what is stable in the midst of renewal. If the bishops are not imaginative or charismatic enough to think through a new rationale in a new direction for Catholic schools, then the priests and religious who constitute the faculties of these schools will be too confused and too frightened to search for new directions.

Finally, Catholic scholars have failed in one of the two critical missions of intellectuals. The intellectual criticizes existing models of behavior and provides alternative models. The Catholic journalists, who presently occupy the places which in more mature Churches would be occupied by scholars, have done a superb job of criticizing the old models but have resolutely refused to consider the possibility of new models. They say that Catholic schools are worthless and that no self-respecting Catholic liberal would send his children to Catholic schools. Therefore, they must be phased out, even if six million children attend them. As for asking whether there may be new directions for Catholic schools in the closing decades of the twentieth century, or whether there may be a unique Catholic contribution to the American educational enterprise, such issues are not even deemed worthy of discussion.

The hierarchy lacked the creativity and the imagination; the clergy lacked the courage and the conviction, and the intellectual leadership lacked the wisdom to provide a new rationale for Catholic schools. With the collapse of the old defensive, protectionist rationale of the Counter-Reformation and the immigrant Church, there seemed nothing for Catholic educators to do but to give up. To talk about searching for a new rationale was merely to talk about preserving an antiquated and outmoded institution. They seemed to be saying, "Even if Catholic schools could make important contributions to American society and the American Church, we should not be asking that question because Catholic schools are outmoded and old-fashioned and are going to be phased out." In other words, Catholic educators gave up the fight even before it began.

The final outcome of present developments is still obscure. There may arise a leadership, a clergy and an intelligentsia who are willing to think about new directions, about construction as well as destruction, about positive possibilities instead of failures and defeats. If they do not, Catholic schools cannot survive their loss of nerve and their collapse of confidence. Under such circumstances the judgment of history will be not that Catholic education was crushed by a hostile non-Catholic society, nor that it was abandoned by an uninterested Catholic population, but rather that it committed suicide.

2. Towards a Theology of Catholic Education

In the previous chapter I said that the principal problem of Catholic education is a collapse of morale, a loss of nerve based on the absence of a theoretical perspective which would give direction and purpose to the Catholic educational system. Catholic educators themselves have lost confidence in what they are doing because they are not able to fit their efforts into some larger system of values. The old rationale may have been good enough for its time, but it is no longer adequate, and a new rationale has not yet been evolved.

In this chapter I intend to make some theological reflections on purposes that Catholic education might serve in a post-Vatican, post-immigrant era. These reflections which can only be considered the crudest sort of beginnings of a theology of Catholic education, are based largely on the research done since the Vatican Council by the great European theologians who write for the theological journal, *Concilium*. In the present chapter, I will attempt to synopsize briefly some of their ideas about the nature of the Church that seem to me particularly pertinent in any consideration of Catholic schools, and I will attempt a preliminary application of these ideas in the work that might be done in Catholic schools.

Let us begin with a series of propositions:

> In his spiritual existence, man will always have to fall back on a sacred mystery as the very ground of his being. This mystery which was in its inexpressible and therefore undefined perimeter permanently contains and sustains the small area of our knowing and doing in our daily experience. Our perception

of reality and our free activity lies at the very root of our being. It is self-evident, but by the same token most hidden and unheeded. It speaks through its silence and its presence, and through its absence it shows us our limitations. We call this God. . . . At the ground of the individual's existence involved in perception and action the sacred mystery that we call God is most deeply within us and at the same time so far beyond us that it does not need us.[1]

In other words, our daily life is rooted in a Reality which, we perceive however dimly, goes beyond our daily life. Indeed, it goes even beyond our own limited reality and represents that on which everything else depends. Whether we acknowledge it or not, and by whatever name we call it, this root of our being still exists and demands our commitment. Man, therefore, lives rooted in God.

However hard and uncertain it may be for us to interpret this deeply and totally primordial experience in the ground of our being, man nevertheless experiences it in his most inward development, that this silent, infinitely distant, sacred mystery, always pointing to the limitations of his finite being and reviewing his guilt, allows him nevertheless to approach it. It enfolds him in an ultimate and radical love, which meets him as salvation and is the real meaning of his existence, as long as he allows the possibility in his love to be wider than his own limitation in guilt. Not only, therefore, are we conscious that we are rooted in a Being beyond our beings, but we also understand that this Being is not merely Being, but also Love, a Love powerfully and overwhelmingly directed at us, and which becomes salvation for us so long as we are brave enough and consonant enough not to flee from it. God gives us not only being, but communicates himself to us in love. This communication of God in love is called

[1] Karl Rahner, "In Search of a Short Formula," *Concilium* (March, 1967), p. 39.

grace. It is offered to all as Light and is the promise
of eternal life. It works freely and graciously in
every man from the primordial source of existence.[2]

Human history must be viewed as a process through which God's
loving nearness becomes more and more manifest to men. God
communicates himself to us in the very beginning and then, despite
all the anguish and tragedy of history, continues to communicate
himself to us.

It is true that this process is often thwarted and
obscured from the history of that guilt incurred by
men when in the mystery of his refusal, he locks
out God's grace and limits himself to an exclusively
self-centered understanding. Yet the process is at
work everywhere and always because the mystery
of the God who reveals and communicates himself
in love is more powerful than the mystery of human
guilt. The historical climax of this self-communication and self-revelation of God to man occurred in
the advent of the God-man, of that man in whom
God was most fully present, Jesus of Nazareth. He
is the fullest communication of God to man that has
occurred, for it is Jesus of Nazareth who is the
ultimate experience of the radical meaning of our
being, of our being subject to death, and of God's
ultimate acceptance.[3]

Jesus, then, is the most concrete and dramatic manifestation of
God's love for us. He who has experienced God in Christ—must
confess Him. For he who has experienced Jesus of Nazareth realizes
that in the dilemma of death versus resurrection, resurrection triumphs; in the dilemma of hope versus despair, hope triumphs; in the
dilemma of tragedy versus comedy, comedy triumphs. Jesus came
to communicate God's life and to communicate it without end. The
Christian who believes in Christ crucified accepts death, but since

[2] *Ibid.*
[3] *Ibid.*

he also believes in Christ risen, he hopefully accepts and expects resurrection.

The goal of salvation history . . .

> has become the recognition of Jesus of Nazareth as the ultimate in God's self-communication. The working out of this salvation history is entrusted to the community of those that are gathered around Jesus in faith, who expect to share in His fulfillment and hope, and who in Him are linked with the Father and one another through His spirit in love. This community is called the Church. It is the Church's task to represent Him and to bear witness to Him in history until the end, so that He will remain and operate in constantly new ways within the concrete process of history as the pledge of God's self-communication.[4]

God communicates Himself first of all through our very being, then through the anguished process of history, then through His ultimate manifestation in the life, death and resurrection of Jesus, and now through the Church. However inadequate, the Church is the community of those committed to Jesus and is to represent him in the world to come.

> The Christian knows his life must be an active expression of unconditional love of God in this hell of men, a love that is the overriding fulfillment of all law. He is consoled by the hope that when his own life and the history of mankind draw to an end, all others, the loved ones, will see in unveiled fulfillment what has already been given in faith and humility, namely the life of God who is all in all. With us the final self-communication of God will come at the end of life and the end of history. The process, begun through being itself, carried on by history, by the theophany in Jesus and by the

[4] Edward Schillebeeckx, "The Church and Mankind," *Concilium* (January, 1965), pp. 34–49.

Church, will be consummated in the total and
perpetual communication of God who is all in all.
The Christian is the man who lives in the midst of
all of these as yet incomplete self-communications
of God. He is a man who lives in faith that the
communication of God's love will be fulfilled, in
hope that he can somehow or the other make a
contribution to the fulfillment of God's promise and
in love which is the beginning here and now of
fulfillment. The Church, then is the sacrament of
mankind's unity. . . .[5]

God communicated himself not merely to individual man but to
a whole race, a race which is united by common origins and common humanity, which from its very beginnings has desperately
sought unity, though it has also been desperately afraid of it. It is
man's guilt and sinfulness which prevents the biological community
of mankind from becoming a fully human communion, and it is
God's love overcoming sin and guilt which makes communion possible. And it is the Church, which however imperfectly represents
the ultimate in God's self-communication, that is, his commission
to lead mankind towards greater communion.

. . . Mankind's new fundamental but real unity . . .
rests upon God's universal saving will. This will is
not an actuality that is simple beyond history. It
has manifested itself visibly within history in the
object of redemption, that is, in the personal life
of Jesus, representative man, Son of God, appearing
among us in our history.[6]

Jesus came into the world, then, to reconvene the human race, to
form a new people, not just a single nation such as Israel but the
whole nation of man bound together in trust, acceptance and love.
The Church, as inadequate as it frequently may be, is both symbol
and agent in this reconvening of mankind. It is, therefore, the people

[5] *Ibid.*
[6] *Ibid.*

of God because God has convened it and because it exists to call other men to a new community of love.

Another way of putting this is to say that the Church is not only a people, but it is a Messianic people. God's self-communication means communion and reunion for the human race through Christ crucified and risen. It is not merely a community that has been convened by faith in the resurrection to enjoy the life of God that Jesus has brought. It is also the community to whom he has been deputed to communicate the good news of mankind's communion and reunion, and to be by word and example God's agent in the creation of the whole communion of mankind. The Church is a Messianic people because it is a people anointed to bring unity and salvation to mankind.

> The incarnation teaches us that the entire human reality can be assumed into a God-centered life. Day to day human life with its wordly concerns for human advancement is the area wherein normal Christian life must develop. The explicit and ecclesial expression of self-communion with God shall indeed be the fountainhead, the driving force of the expression of Christian life in the world. Improving the world whenever we improve ourselves, we are always in the presence of and beneath the wings of the mystery who gives himself freely.[7]

Or, to put the matter somewhat differently, even though the world is creature, is non-God and is, therefore, blighted by sin, imperfection, and its profane, earthly and temporal reality, it does have it's own special and immediate ends. And it will be assumed through Christ into the absolute and gratuitous presence of God. The Christian cannot communicate with God without communicating with other men. He realizes that his unity with other men is ultimately rooted in God's unifying power, but also that this unity must be worked out through a long, slow, agonizing process of improving human relationships.

[7] Yves Congar, *The Church That I Love* (Wilkes-Barre, Pa.: Dimension Books, Inc., 1969).

Christianity means not only communion with God and the concrete reality of Christ and His Church, but also working with the living God, with the Father who is ever active both in the Church and in the world. Religion is primarily personal intercourse with God, the living God who is the Creator of men and things, all of which He offers to us for humanization. Therefore, our living relationship with our neighbor and with the world is not only cultural but also religious. . . .[8]

Agape embraces God and men. . . .

Love of God cannot and must not be separated from love of men. Christian love for the neighbor means that we—God and I—love my fellowmen, while the natural human love, God, is present only in silence as transcended Third. My Christian *charitas* toward my fellow is just as much love, but a love lived in communion with God, and so the Christian loves his fellowmen because they are loved by God. In Christ alone do we learn the proper meaning of being a man for the sake of others, although secular and human experience will teach us how we must express this fellowship in concrete situations.[9]

If we pause at this point and try to summarize the contributions of Rahner, Schillebeeckx and Congar, we must say that three points seem of critical importance:

God communicates himself to us through being, through history, through Jesus and through the Church.

The Church has been appointed to continue the communication of God through Jesus in time and space to the rest of mankind so that man might be reconvened in community and love.

The Christian responds to his vocation, not by withdrawing from

8 Schillebeeckx, *The Church and Mankind*, p. 40.
9 *Ibid*. p. 48.

human relationships and from human culture but by giving himself over to the rest of mankind in service and love, a service and love which are deepened and enriched by his awareness that through Jesus human relationships and human culture have been assumed into the process of resurrection.

In this theological perspective there is absolutely no room for a Christian to withdraw from the world. (Even those Christians who go to the monastery in a radical way remain part of the world.) Human relationships, human activities, human cultures have not only immense value in themselves, but they have super added value because they are the ways through which mankind is slowly reconvened in unity in Christ Jesus.

While the existentialist influence on the European theologians is obvious, one must also emphasize the fact that they are all profoundly influenced by their predecessor, Pierre Teilhard de Chardin, who saw the evolution of the human race towards self-fulfillment as being the same process as the evolution of God's people towards the parousia. If the God who creates is the same as the God who redeems, and if the process begun with the incarnation and the resurrection is merely a continuation of the self-communication of God that began in creation, then the programs which inch mankind towards fulfillment and the Church towards parousia, are in reality the same voyage to the same Omega point.

Three more propositions must be added to our theological sketch:

The Church, like all people, has an organization. It is not only the people of God; it is the body of Christ, to use Father Yves Congar's phrase. It is organized into structures and institutions. The fact that it is organized is rooted in its humanness, since all human communities require organization. Hence, the hierarchical structure of the Church can be said to be part of its basic nature. The mere fact of structure does not distinguish the Church from other human societies which also require structure as part of their basic nature. While some basic outlines of the structure of the Church may well be immutable, most of the patterns and relationships that we call ecclesiastical structure are changeable and need to be changed to meet the different challenges and opportunities which the Church encounters as the world about it changes.

At the present time the emphasis on the reforming of structures in the Church frequently makes it seem that some critics have lost sight of the important role that structure and organization play in all human communities. But it is clear to the sociologists that leadership is required for coordination, for unity, for symbolizing goals, for keeping the attention of the membership upon critical values to which the community is committed, and for asking the pertinent questions which will disturb the members of the community out of their complacency and inertia. In other words, organization and structure are intended to be assets rather than liabilities.

But if the Church does require, like all human communities, order and organization, it is also charismatic, that is, it is committed to the notion that the Holy Spirit speaks not merely through its official leaders, but also through the talents, abilities and insights of its members. Indeed, one of the most critical tasks of leadership is to distinguish among the charisma which it observes and hears.

The *Dogmatic Constitution on the Church* of the Second Vatican Council makes explicit the fact that the whole Christian people is anointed by the Holy Spirit.

The Church celebrates and ratifies its unity through its liturgy, particularly through the Eucharist,

> the sacred meal of Christ's community, where this community commemorates salvation and the death and resurrection of its Lord and constantly renews its union with its Lord in a ritual meal under the sign of bread and wine. This ratification of unity in external ceremony represents the Church's commitment to its conviction that it possesses self-communication of God in Jesus Christ, and its joy that communion with Christ is made possible among men through his triumph over fear, hatred and death.[10]

This brief sketch of the developments of postconciliar theology is not intended to be a complete or exhaustive synthesis of the theological work that has been done in Europe since the Council.

[10] Cf. Hans Kung, "The Charismatic Structure of the Church," *Concilium* (April, 1965).

It is intended to provide a background for our remarks about the goals of Catholic education. The writers on whom we have relied in the preparation of this chapter have not explicitly—as far as I know—treated the subject of Catholic schools. Therefore, they could be quite properly offended if it were thought that I was using their authority to theologize about Catholic schools. All I will suggest is that it is possible to use this postconciliar theology as a basis for shaping a new rationale for Catholic schools.

New Directions for Catholic Education

In this section I intend to outline the beginnings of a specific theology of Catholic education within the context of the previous chapter. I want to make it quite explicit that this is a theoretical rather than an empirical exercise. In lectures I have said some of the things that I will propose here and the reaction has usually been, "What you talk about is fine in theory; the only trouble is that it really doesn't work in Catholic schools."

The only trouble with such a questioner is that he is incapable of participating in a discussion of Catholic education which is not bound in the framework of being for or against Catholic schools. Therefore, when someone attempts to chart a direction in which Catholic education might go, the questioner is forced to say, "There is no point in trying to chart that direction because we're not there yet."

Even though it must seem self-evident, one must say that if one is charting directions, one obviously assumes that the institution for which the direction is being charted has not yet arrived at the new goal. Furthermore, since we are dealing with a human institution, it is very likely that it will never perfectly achieve the theoretical goals outlined for it. The relevant operational question is not, "Are the goals which I will outline in this section actually now being achieved in Catholic schools?" It is not even, "Can Catholic schools achieve these goals perfectly in the foreseeable future?" It is the much more simple question, "Is it possible for Catholic schools to move in these directions?" To this question I must reply that I do not see any reason why we cannot.

My remarks about theoretical directions for Catholic education can be subsumed under three headings: innovation, love and comedy.

Innovation

The theologians cited in the last chapter argue almost unanimously that God communicates himself to us through history. Although the historical and cultural processes have a goal and value of their own, they also have a transcendent purpose in the fact of Christ's incarnation. The Christian must, therefore, be deeply involved in the human pilgrimage toward self-fulfillment because he realizes it is the same journey as that of the people of God towards the parousia. Although a Christian aims for a goal that transcends human culture, it is not a goal which negates human culture nor one which destroys it. It will in the final reconciliation transform it.

Now it seems safe to assume that education is one of the most important cultural activities in which men engage for through the educational process they try to pass on their culture to the generation after them and also to expand and enrich the cultural heritage.

If the Church is committed to the role of leader of man's pilgrimage, it seems appropriate, though surely not absolutely necessary, that the Church be involved in education, not to defend or protect the faith of its members, but to bear witness to its conviction of mankind's destiny by taking the lead in mankind's educational progress. So an appropriate goal for Catholic education would be the task of "research and development." Catholic educators should be leaders in educational innovation.

Many non-Catholic educators are astonished that this has not already happened. They argue that Catholic schools are likely to get far more popular support outside the Church if they do take the lead in innovation, and that since the Catholic schools do not have to contend with legislatures, school boards, trustees and massive educational bureaucracies, they have much greater flexibility to innovate.

These colleagues may underestimate the amount of organizational inertia within the American Church, but I think that they are right. There is more freedom to innovate within Catholic schools. If Catholic educators have the will to seize this freedom, they can move forward rapidly. The spectacular educational developments at some Catholic colleges such as Immaculate Heart and Barat, are sufficient evidence that it is possible for Catholic schools to become impressive leaders in the innovation process. I believe that religious orders provide a base and a core for innovative style which is a tremendous help to a school which wants to experiment. If Catholic schools have not taken the leadership in innovation, it is partly out of timidity and partly because of self-hatred. Catholic educators for the past twenty years have tried to catch up with the rest of American education. Now some of them, in the vernacular of our time, have decided that they ought to do their own thing. It's high time.

What kinds of innovation are most appropriate for Catholic schools? The four educational propositions I mentioned in the first section can be summarized in one sentence: all education is self-education, but is best achieved in community and through interpersonal relationships. Given its commitment to the dignity of the total human person and its belief in salvation for body as well as soul, the Church ought to have special sympathy for those four propositions and ought to be in the vanguard of those who want to break out of the compartments into which education has placed the different dimensions of the human personality. Furthermore, since Catholic schools are affiliated with parishes, religious orders and dioceses, they have links to the world beyond the school that are not available to other educational institutions. Therefore, Catholic education has the theoretical and practical resources to break out of the existing educational categories.

Education for Individual Development

The approach of the so-called "education for individual development" schools with their emphasis on the development of the total human personality ought to be especially interesting to Catholic educators who have always insisted on the need to "educate the whole man." Unfortunately, education of the whole man has frequently meant for Catholic schools that in addition to the standard curriculum, there is also a religion course and compulsory attendance at Church services or religious exercises. This is surely a narrow notion of education of the whole man. But the harmony between the theoretical statements about integrating the development of the total human personality and the approach of the so-called "developmental" school is so obvious that one would assume that Catholic educators could ignore it only with great difficulty.

Education of the Whole Family

Research on Catholic schools done at the National Opinion Research Center strongly documents what most teachers know to be true from their personal experience. The school is effective only when the school and the family reinforce one another. It follows that for education of children to be effective, the rest of the family must be involved. American educators have not even begun to face the implications of such a conclusion, though the relevance of this conclusion to the problems of the inner city should be obvious. But because Catholic schools are integrated into a larger ecclesiastical system, they ought to have much better access to parents than any other schools. The failure of Catholic schools to devote more attention to education of the whole family is hard to understand. It seems an opportunity too good to be missed.

Education for Community Service

From the very beginning of Catholic education in the United States, Church leaders have argued that Catholic schools exist in part to train a lay leadership for the Church. Statistical data suggest that this goal has been reasonably well accomplished. But after the Second Vatican Council lay leadership began to mean something more than it had in the past. Today it means not merely laymen who are involved in the internal problems of the Church, but also laymen who are deeply involved in the problems of society. Catholic schools, therefore, ought to ask what it takes to educate an elite of committed citizens who believe that their special education demands of them a special involvement in the problems of the world around them. The use of the very word, "elite," annoys some superficial enthusiasts in Catholic education because they can conceive of no other elite except an elite of special privilege. But what we are discussing is not an elite of special privilege, but an elite of special obligation.

Education Through Community Involvement

The volunteer movement of the 1960's was an extraordinary educational opportunity which has been vulgarized by a number of American educators. Students are not likely to change society, but students' involvement in social problems is not likely to improve their learning experience if the educational implications of such involvement are ignored. Far too many educators seem persuaded that merely by sending students into the inner city for a quarter of a semester great social reforms and great educational achievements will be produced. From assuming that everything can be learned in the classroom, they have assumed that nothing can be learned in the classroom.

Most Catholic schools have ignored the advantages of linking the classroom with life. They have also failed to use an extraordinarily important educational resource—the worldwide network of Catholic social service agencies. Catholic schools have many assets which they have not chosen to use perhaps because so many Catholic educators have been wallowing in their identity crises.

Opportunities abound for Catholic educators who wish to lead in educational innovation. If they seize these opportunities, by the end of the present century no one will ask whether there is any point in having Catholic schools. If they do not seize them, I will admit that Catholic schools should go out of business.

Love

Jesus has told us, "By this all men will know that you are my disciples, if you have love for one another" (John 13:35). The theologians cited previously emphasized that the self-communication of God is a self-communication in love, and it is by loving one's fellowmen that Catholics principally exercise their role as messianic people. Furthermore, educational research suggests that Plato was right when he indicated that the teacher-student relationship is a relationship of love. It is not love, indeed, as it is between a husband and wife, but it is still love because the teacher uses his person to win over the student.

Now, if education is ultimately a love relationship and if the Church is committed to human love, Catholic schools should be distinguished by the quality and amount of the love among the various participants in the educational enterprise. That it may not always be so is undeniable, but it is equally undeniable that sometimes it is so. Research on the ability of high schools to integrate the intellectually, emotionally or financially disadvantaged into the life of the school shows that in some instances charity very definitely has been present in Catholic schools.

I was once asked to help draft a statement on Catholic schooling for a group of bishops. I made the point that because of the Church's commitment to love, the teachers in Catholic schools ought to be better lovers than teachers at other schools. One of my colleagues on the committee laughingly said, "You don't think you can get the bishops to agree that teachers in Catholic schools ought to be lovers, do you? It would almost be as difficult," he continued, "to persuade the bishops to admit that they ought to be lovers." "By this all men will know that you are my disciples . . ." (John 13:35).

How badly can we miss the point?

To say that there ought to be more love in Catholic schools is merely to open the issue. I have no idea what kinds of personal and social growth would be necessary to make this goal a reality, but it does seem that it's a goal of such overriding importance that Catholic educators should devote their energy to creating love.

One would also assume the Catholic commitment to love would make it necessary for the Catholic schools, faculty, administrators and students alike, to be deeply involved in serving Christ where he is to be found among the poor. "Truly, I say to you, as you did it to one of the least of these my brethren, you did it to me" (Mt. 25:40). Catholic educators in the inner city schools must spend large amounts of time and energy to keep the schools solvent. Yet, the Church should realize that the opportunity for Christian service in the inner city is so important and so dramatic that much greater expenditure of resources in these schools is imperative. Once again,

Catholics have failed to recognize their own strength or even their own accomplishments.

Finally, with respect to love, it seems reasonable to assume that Catholic education could legitimately concern itself with the problems of human sexuality. The Freudian revolution which finally overturned three thousand years of the Platonistic-Manichean tradition is one of the great phenomena of the twentieth century because it is now clear that the human body is not evil and that human sexuality does not subvert man. Man is not a spirit imprisoned in body. He is a psychosomatic composite, and his sexuality, which is so obviously and disturbingly corporeal, is a powerful force. It can destroy, but it can also liberate him for self-fulfillment. One would think the Catholic church would rejoice in this revolution because it has always been committed to the idea that man was a psychosomatic composite and not a spirit imprisoned in a body. Scripture tells us that Jesus came to preach life to the whole man, not salvation for only the soul. The union between man and woman is, in both the Old Testament and New, the pervasive symbol of the love between Christ and his Church.

In the Easter liturgy the Church reforms what is obviously an intercourse ritual when the lighted candle is plunged into the waters to symbolize the fact that through the resurrection Christ consummated his marriage with his beloved spouse, the Church. In the present Easter liturgy the very words indicate the sexual nature of the ritual: "May this candle fructify these waters."

As H. Marshall McLuhan has pointed out, sex is not yet "cool." It is still isolated from the rest of human life. It is not integrated into human existence so that it may pervade it in a more relaxed and casual way than it has in the past. The Freudian revolution has been dramatic, but neither human wisdom nor human behavior has been able to assimilate it. One would suppose that Catholicism, with the richness of sexuality in its tradition, would be in the forefront of those human institutions which are trying to assimilate the Freudian revolution. That we have not yet taken the lead in doing so is not necessarily a sign that we cannot.

In many parts of the country there are now fierce controversies about sex education in the schools. For the most part they are mindless controversies. Catholics who are so adamantly opposed to sex education in Catholic schools are quite unaware of, and would be terrified by the pervasive sexuality of the scriptural and liturgical traditions of the Roman Church. But Catholic educators who respond to these attacks by permitting the questions to be focused on whether courses on how babies are born should be given in the classroom have missed the point, too. The real issue is the question of the role of sexuality in human life. This is a broad, pervasive question which cannot be discussed in merely one course. And it probably cannot be discussed without considerable personal growth in most teachers. Obviously, we cannot expect Catholic schools to become instantaneously successful in communicating proper attitudes towards human sexuality. On the other hand, the goal of providing young people with a much more sophisticated understanding of their own sexuality is one for which Catholic schools are singularly well suited. If even moderate progress is made toward this goal before the end of the century, no one will question the appropriateness of Catholic schools in the year 2,000.

Comedy

Under the title of "Comedy" we subsume the behavior of men attempting to transcend the mundane routine of everyday life. One of the most dramatic cultural changes of our time is the attempt of increasing numbers of American people to escape the rationalized, computerized, bureaucratized, formalized, secularized society in which they live. The move to the suburbs was an attempt, however unsuccessful, of one generation to get back to nature. Drugs, rock music and hippie communes are the more sophisticated attempts of a later generation, though ones that are no more likely to be successful.

Modern secular man is becoming aware once again that he is irrevocably linked to the primordial processes of the universe and that he can ignore these processes only at great peril to himself. Myths, ritual, mysticism and ecstasy were human activities that cannot be dispensed with merely because we have invented a television set, a jet airplane or even the electric light. Authors like Robert Neale in his book, *In Praise of Play** and Sam Keen in his *Apology for Wonder*** insist that only by breaking free of the limitations of the workaday world and giving oneself over to play, to wonder, adventure, excitement and delight can man reestablish contact with the primordial life forces of the universe. When one says, "primordial life forces of the universe," one is but a step away from speaking of the Force which underpins all other forces and a Being who is the Creator of all other beings. Surely in the search for myths, mysticism and ecstasy, man is looking once again for the Transcendent.

There is a good deal of foolishness and unintelligent enthusiasm for the "turning on" approach to reality. But because some of the devotees of "turning on" go to ridiculous extremes, it does not follow that the new search for the playful and the comic as preludes to the mystic and the ecstatic is unsound or inappropriate. Quite the contrary. From the Catholic viewpoint the quest for comedy ought to be a matter of great rejoicing.

Yet how much comedy is there in Catholic education? How much playfulness in Catholic schools? Or, for that matter, how much mysticism or ecstasy? Has the master of a 2,000-year-old tradition of liturgy and mysticism so lost touch with its own traditional resources that it is unable to respond to the present quest to transcend the mundane? Is it desacralizing itself at precisely the time when the rest of the country seems to be looking once again for the sacred? Are we exploring the secular city at the very time that Harvey Cox is in the suburbs celebrating the eucharistic assembly in praise of play, folly and wonder? Once again we seem bent upon ignoring the best of our own resources in our foolish attempts to be like everybody else was five years ago.

Yet if Catholic education could become authentically playful, indeed, authentically comic, there would be no question by the end of the present century whether there was a uniquely Catholic contribution to education. Whether or not we can make our unique contribution may be an irrelevant question. The pertinent question is, "Should we do it?" If we should, then we will.

* New York: Harper & Row, 1969.
** New York: Harper & Row, 1969.

Love, innovation and the comic are enough goals for any educational system and sufficient challenges for Catholic education today. The pessimism, self-hatred, cynicism and despair which is so characteristic of the Catholic educational scene at the present time ought to yield quickly to such challenges if men and women have courage and creativity to face them.

Part 2.

*Christian Approaches
to Catholic Education*

William E. Brown

3. The Redefinition of Purpose

Any venture that succeeds must have a worthwhile purpose, and the purpose must be understood by all who are engaged in it and by all who are served or affected by it. Unless all participants understand and appreciate the goals, they will not be able to act intelligently and effectively to support and to fulfill the venture's purpose.

Three possible reasons may explain a project's failure: the need it was designed to meet no longer exists; the need still exists but the project is not meeting it because it has not maintained the quality of its performance or improved it to meet changed conditions; or the need still exists but it is no longer understood or appreciated by those engaged in the work or served by it. The latter two explanations may coexist in a cause-and-effect relationship.

Without question Catholic education is in a serious decline. It is unnecessary to cite the recent 20% drop in Catholic grade and high school enrollment to prove it, or to point to the failure of CCD programs, or to mention the slender efforts to mount adult education programs, much less the failure to get adults interested enough to attend them. Most of us refer to the situation as a "crisis."

Loss of Sense of Purpose

Confusion abounds as to why the situation exists and what to do about it. It is not the normal type of confusion that accompanies adjustments in school curricula and schedules, which always arises

49

out of self-criticism and experimentation. That kind of confusion is mechanical, and it is a sign of vitality rather than mortal illness. The confusion affecting the Catholic community with respect to education is deadlier. It hits rational animals who have lost their way and are overcome first by panic and then despair. The "in" word for this is "anomie," a breakdown or absence of norms or values.

Education is the process of learning by which the individual makes of himself what he wishes to be in the context of his society and culture. He can achieve this by observing, listening, reflecting and acting. But every civilized society, and certainly our present one, has provided formal educational assistance to its people, or at least selected classes of its people. Society provides schools, not only for the good of the individual, but also for the good of society, because it is considered in the common good for members of the community to have a high level of learning.

In our country a substantial amount of public funds is spent on a system of education beginning with preschool children and extending through elementary schools, secondary schools and colleges into adult life, with various special schools for vocational training at teen-age and adult levels. Whether or not the system is achieving its purpose is beside our point for the moment. (This question will be given some consideration in Chapter 4.) The system was designed to provide excellent facilities for everything people need to learn to fulfill their goals in our socially, economically and technologically advanced society—with one singular exception. Under our constitutions (states as well as federal) it is unlawful for religion, or moral values presented as religious values, to be taught in our publicly financed school system. Education in religion and religion-based moral values is left to the home, the churches, privately financed schools and the individuals themselves.

The Catholic Church is the chief organization which established private schools to provide an education designed to include religion and religious values. At great effort and expense, the Catholic Church in our country maintains schools which in 1969 served nearly half of the Catholic children of elementary school age, nearly a third of those of high school age and nearly a sixth of those of college age. In addition, formal programs exist for teaching religion and religious values to Catholic children who attend public grade and high schools, and less formal programs for those who attend public colleges. The Catholic schools constitute the backbone of our educational venture.

Although the Catholic community has constructed and maintained schools for over a hundred years, it appears that many of us have now forgotten the basic purposes and specific goals of these institutions. Others have lost confidence in those purposes and goals. Still others have become uncertain whether Catholic schools justify the sacrifices which they assume will be required to maintain them. Finally, many who would be willing to make those sacrifices are afraid that not enough other people are equally willing to do so. The debunkers are found chiefly among certain intellectuals; the fearful and the despairing are found chiefly among the ordinary laity, and among the ordinaries.

The bishops' November 16, 1967, Statement on Catholic Education did little to dispel this anomie. Since then, the bishops (as a group) have said little of significance about the subject. More will be said about that Statement in chapter 5 of this book. For the moment, let me say only that the Statement contained more commitment than conviction. It was a dogged promise to 6 million children and their parents and an exhortation to a quarter of a million teachers. It contained little about why the commitment should be continued, much less extended to more millions of children, and nothing about how the commitment was to be met. The bishops confessed that they did not know how it was to be met and promised merely a research program to find out. They promised a two- or three-year research program instead of a number of practical things that could have been done at once, observable common sense things which a research program would only have verified. This is anomie at the highest level.

None of the meetings, seminars or discussions of the grade and high school situation has ended on a positive note about the value of our schools or the possibility of updating them. Discouragement about updating, however, is always demonstrated by lack of confidence in our ability to provide adequate finances and by our unwillingness to break with our traditional country-store kind of administration. However, we seem to be sure we can update course content and pedagogical know-how, even though we do argue about curricula and teaching methods.

In one such symposium five eminent educators, clerical and lay, discussed Catholic education before an audience of 1,500 parents and teachers. The community, like every other community which has a substantial investment in Catholic grade and high schools, was disturbed about the existing situation and was seeking guidance. One of the experts actually suggested that the Catholic schools are un-American because they are divisive and undemocratic. Not one of them, in answer to a question from the audience, would say what the special value of Catholic schools is, or what superiority or even significant difference parents or society should expect from the results of Catholic school education as distinguished from public school education. Not one suggested ways to get adequate financing. On the contrary, the tone of the panel on this all-important point was discouraging to the point of hopelessness.

One thing was certain and one thing probable about that symposium. A dispiriting atmosphere from the ivory tower on stage swept over the audience. And probably most of the teaching sisters in the audience, who had sponsored the program, went back to their convent that night baffled and anguished. The parents were baffled and angry.

With a few notable exceptions, the reports in the Catholic press about who is saying what about these matters are depressing. Too many people involved in Catholic education seem to be cowed by certain intellectuals who day in and day out peddle the doctrine that the schools are passé and should be phased out. Is it any wonder that school enrollment, which should increase at a rate at least equal to population increase—about 1.2% a year—has been declining since 1965 at an accelerating rate, averaging about 5% a year? The depopulation of our schools seems to be snowballing. If the trend continues, what seems to be the fondest hope of the ivory tower intellectuals will be realized in a few short years. The only remaining schools will be a few run for the benefit and at the expense of a wealthy elite. Would this elite allow its schools to teach the quality of Christianity envisioned by Vatican II?

It is shocking to learn that the schools that are being "phased out" are inner city schools which have the largest enrollment. Surely we have lost our way when we deliberately abandon the poorest of the poor. It is hardly less reprehensible when, as has been done in some places, instead of closing inner city schools we spin them off from the Church, with publicly proclaimed "generosity," into the hands of those among the poor who are willing to try to operate them with "freedom" and "independence" and to support them with their own meager resources and what they can beg from others.

What message can possibly come through to these poor people and the poor communities among whom they live, except that the Church is not interested in them because they drain off too much energy and money? They must know that there is no reason why the Church could not devise programs, or permit experimentation, including some form of participation by the local community, to keep their schools open. The poor surely know that the Catholic Church *could* do this within its own structures and *should* do it because it has a God-mandated mission to the poor. The faith and courage of these poor people in undertaking these schools holds up to shame before God and men the lack of charity and generosity of the people and their leaders who proclaim themselves to be the people of God, Christ present in the world. In the face of such evidence, who will say that we do not need to recover our sense of purpose with respect to the schools?

Alleged Shortcomings and Failures of the Schools

We must bring the discussion of the whys and hows of Catholic education out of the narrow confines of the ivory tower and beyond the research studies of pre-Vatican II Catholic education. We must conduct the discussion in the atmosphere of everyday life and post-Vatican II Catholic educational purposes and goals.

What about the charge that we have not derived from Catholic education what we hoped our vast commitment of resources to it would produce? We got from our expenditures exactly what we hoped to get when we established our schools. We got identity. This is no more and no less than the recent research studies showed us we got out of it. But suddenly the intellectuals have become disenchanted with that identity because it is not "ecumenical minded" and "socially conscious." These experts are, of course, examining it with the 20-20 vision of post-Vatican II hindsight, just like the rest of us; only they are pretending they knew it all the time. The intellectually honest position is that we have learned a lot in the years since Vatican II, not so much about teaching methods as about purposes and goals. It is manifestly dishonest to blame the schools for lacking the spirit of *aggiornamento* and all that that term implies before they so much as heard the word. None of us heard the word until Pope John dropped it into the placid pond upon which the bark of Peter with its crew and passengers was floating.

Then there is the charge that the schools are ghettoish, divisive, even un-American. A certain intellectual stated that a ghetto is a subcommunity imposed by others or self-imposed, turned in upon itself voluntarily or by force, having no concern for or allowed to have no part in the larger community. This is bad. But the larger community is by nature composed of many subcommunities which provide their members with identity; and only when a person has achieved identity is he a whole person and a help to others, including those in the larger community. This is good. Yet, said this gentleman: a Catholic subcommunity is bad. At least, the use of a Catholic school system is bad because it is divisive; it is self-imposed ghettoism.

Shouldn't this gentleman, considering his premises, have said that a Catholic school system is the ideal way to provide Catholic children (as members of a sub-community) with identity? Logic would demand that he admit that a Catholic school system would be good, provided only that its viewpoint was not only inward but also outward and that its educational aims were to teach students what it is to be a Catholic, and if possible, to inculcate personal commitment to be a Catholic and to enter and serve the larger community as a Catholic.

The contention that our schools are divisive and un-American is astonishing. It contradicts, of course, the contention that the schools do not form children to be "different." Neither charge is just. The schools should make children "different." And the right to be different, and the right of parents to form children to be different in religious or cultural beliefs and practices, is the essence of Americanism. Persons who accuse the Catholic schools of violating Americanism show either a lack of assurance about their religious beliefs or a distaste for being different. Since the difference is precisely Catholicism, maybe these persons should graciously retire from the public debate about the schools until they have reassessed their beliefs about Catholicism. Hopefully, they will conclude that authentic Catholicism, the fullness of Christianity, not only is significantly different but also that, if understood and practiced, it would make a vast and beneficial difference in the nation and in the world.

In all justice, however, these critics may be in favor of authentic Catholicism, and they may believe in its significance. But perhaps they have been influenced by the apparent failure of the schools to form outgoing Catholics and by personal doubt that the schools can ever succeed in doing so. But it seems fair to question their common sense if they believe that parents can be turned around more easily than can the school administrators, and suddenly, or even soon enough, parents can be reeducated in post-Vatican II outlooks and insights so as to be able to transmit them to their children.

There is a rash incongruity in the idea that parents—enough parents—can be turned around more easily than the schools. Only persons who live in ivory towers and not in parishes would agree. This idea would certainly not occur to persons who have remained in the parishes, nor to those who have disassociated themselves from geographical parishes and have joined floating parishes. For those who live in parishes, or who have joined a floating parish, have experienced at first hand the multitude of Baltimore Catechism-educated Catholics who not only do not know post-Vatican II Catholic teachings but are not even interested in learning them. They have met many who have not even heard of Vatican II, and not a few who militantly oppose its teachings. How can it reasonably be supposed that these people will suddenly be persuaded to attend adult education courses to prepare themselves to pass Vatican II Catholicism on to their children?

Critics on the ghettoish, divisive, un-American theme should suggest ways to help the schools produce patently "different" children, rather than to phase out the schools.

The Role of Management in Redefining Purpose

We find ourselves in much the same position as a large manufacturing corporation which has had a successful product line for many years and suddenly finds itself confronted with a jolting technological change or a market preference shift which threatens its success. Does it liquidate its assets and go out of business? Does it allow itself to drift downhill into bankruptcy? Not if its management has competence and nerve. The management draws upon all the brainpower at its command, both within and outside the corporation, and engages in a quick, possibly expensive, honest and realistic appraisal of the entire situation.

First, they reexamine the corporation's fundamental purpose. They may find that its purpose is not to manufacture, let us say, gasoline-powered automobiles but to manufacture automobiles however powered. Or it may decide that its basic purpose is to manufacture any vehicle which provides transportation, including helicopters or electric commuter trains.

If the new development is an automobile powered by an electric fuel cell, the problem of updating is fairly simple. The corporation develops a fuel cell of its own or finds an outside supply and makes the necessary adaptations in its automobile chassis and body to substitute the fuel cell for the gasoline engine.

If the technological change or market shift involves electric commuter trains, the problem is greater. Even so, the managers study the corporation's existing resources and facilities and then make necessary changes to convert from automobiles to commuter trains. In either case, they make the necessary changes in product design and facilities, marshal resources of men and money, explain the new purposes and goals to all employes and potential customers, and presently the corporation is rolling along again with a successful new product.

The management of the corporation perceives the change in the outside environment in which the corporation operates, appraises the situation, decides what to do about it, restates the corporation's purposes and goals, makes the practical plans for achieving them, assigns personnel and issues the instructions to carry out the required functions. Analogy between this business example and the school situation is sound enough to demonstrate why it is important to stress the role of management. Management is precisely what our schools do not have. They do not even have a system.

When pressed with suggestions for reformation some diocesan curial officials have said that a diocesan system, meaning schools administered and financed centrally at the diocesan level, and a fortiori a regional or a national system, is contrary to canon law. Whether because of canon law, inertia or personal preference, what we have is actually, and in many cases purposely, a nonsystem.

This situation is basically the result, not of canon law, but of a state of mind. More than any other single factor it will defeat all efforts to update and adequately administer and finance our schools unless we change it. The schools got along fairly well without systematization and centralized management in slower, less complicated, less competitive times. But if they are to survive in the future, they must be systematized and managed.

The assumed crucial difference between management and leadership needs clarification. Leadership has a connotation of the charismatic, the personal, the inspirational about it. Leaders with such qualities are wonderful people to have around when dullards or sluggards need motivating to start or to carry through a difficult venture. In most affairs of life, however, just as an expert is usually an ordinary guy away from home, a leader is usually a reasonably competent manager—at home.

A business, even a huge business, does not need a charismatic leader to be successful. Neither does a school system. Both need good management. That means not just one, but a whole set of reasonably competent managers. Unlike charismatic leadership, management is a profession that does not depend upon a fortunate heredity. It can be learned by men who have certain talents and personality traits, to be sure, but they need no charisms whatever.

It would be fortunate if a leader or two with compelling inspirational ability should appear among our bishops to restate and resell Christian education to the Catholic community. But for the everyday operation that kind of leadership is unnecessary. Good management, on the other hand, is indispensable.

Management is a service. Its function is to make plans and general policy decisions. It has authority to delegate responsibility to carry out the plans and authority to enforce its policy decisions. But management remains a service, answerable to its principals and ultimately subject to their wishes. Furthermore, the wisest management engages those who will be affected by the success or failure of the plans and those who are expected to carry them out in the process of developing, defining and assigning the necessary functions to carry out the plans. In terms of the latest management jargon, it uses the principles of participative management and management by objective.

The Bishops' Role

Applying the foregoing concept of management to the business of Catholic education, we see that parents within the Catholic community primarily, but also the entire Catholic community and, in a related but important way, the entire civic community, are both stockholders and customers of the product of the schools. The administrators and the teachers are the employees. School administrators should consult all these groups to ascertain their needs and ideas and to obtain the broadest possible understanding and agreement about educational goals and then develop the best plans for achieving those goals.

The bishops as a group, like the board of directors of a corporation, have by the nature of their office the role of top management of Catholic education. Each ordinary by the nature of his office has top management responsibility and authority for Catholic education in his diocese, much like a plant manager or a territory sales manager in a business organization. Suggestions on how to carry out these responsibilities will be elaborated in Chapter 5 of this book. In this chapter it is enough to insist the principles of participative management and management by objective be applied at all levels to define purpose and develop the best goals and plans and the greatest possible understanding and enthusiasm of those assigned to carry them out.

Individual bishops here and there say that the responsibility for the religious education of children, even in the schools, belongs to the parents. Parents are being invited, sometimes told, to develop plans and means for maintaining the schools. This is such a change in attitude that most people do not take it seriously. Nor should they until their bishop suggests a practical way for the laity to assume this responsibility.

They will not hear any such extreme suggestions, of course, because the concept is wrong. Catholic education is the bishops' most fundamental responsibility. Christian education, teaching all nations the Word of God and pointing out its applications to the questions and problems of the day is the Church's mission. Christian education is mission; it is the most important mission the Church has. The bishops should consult with and listen to the entire people of God as to "how" to carry on Christian education, but they cannot delegate the responsibility for the "whether" or the major policy decisions as to the "how" to anyone. They must lead, and they must manage the educational mission. This is an absolutely fundamental point not sufficiently stressed in discussions to date. The bishops must take the lead in Catholic education. They must take the lead in solving the school problem because of its nature and because of the nature of their office. No other group can direct the venture and assure its objectives as Catholic mission.

It is difficult to understand why the bishops are not being more inspiring, more active with respect to the schools, and why they are not assuming the leadership needed. Surely it is not because of lack of followers, although they may fear otherwise. At every opportunity in parish meetings or in diocesan meetings, parents have been almost anguished in their pleas for updating the schools. While they plead for more administrative economies to hold down costs, they indicate willingness to foot the bill for any program of assured comprehensiveness, excellence and efficiency. They plead for a program that they can see, to which they can lend support on a rational basis instead of blind faith that "the superintendent of schools has everything under control." Since there are no programs nor any indications that the bishops are interested in developing them, parents are losing faith in the future of the schools and are sadly removing their children from them. The longer the situation is allowed to drift in this aimless way, the more difficult it will be to rebuild a stable system.

The evidence is becoming clearer every day that a significant part of the vocation crisis among teaching orders of religious stems from the same uncertainty about the attitude of the bishops toward the schools. It seems that everyone except the bishops realizes that without the leadership of the bishops there can be no Catholic schools.

It does not seem possible that the bishops are uncertain about the worth of the schools in the Church's teaching mission. It seems more likely that their procrastination is due to uncertainty about the comparative worth of the schools vis-à-vis the difficulties of supporting them. The greater part of this book will be devoted to the problems involved in balancing this equation. We hope that all concerned, particularly the bishops, will find our discussion encouraging, and that it will inspire the bishops to move along the lines suggested. The last thing we need these days is bishops who are dispirited and who have become immobilized through loss of nerve. These are symptoms of the death wish. In the context of the Church's educational problems it would point to loss of faith. Surely our problems are not that deep.

Yet our problems might possibly, just possibly, revolve around the question of what is the Christian faith. If the bishops are undecided about that, their procrastination about the schools is readily explainable because the precise purpose of the schools is to teach the truths and the implications of the truths of the Christian faith. If the bishops are undecided about whether to follow the interpretations and directions spelled out by the bishops of the world almost unanimously in the four years of deliberations of the Second Vatican Council, if they fear that the new interpretations and directions may prove to be hard sayings and drive many members out of the Church, then they will not move strongly in the field of Catholic education until they have resolved that dilemma one way or another.

Christ assuredly did not consider that His teachings drove many people from Him. They left of their own accord. And He let them go. Nor did Christ seem concerned about the immediate statistical success of His mission.

Similarly, the bishops should not be afraid to preach the purer and in many ways tougher brand of Christianity described by Vatican II, even though it may separate the men from the boys in today's pews. Whom would they prefer to see there today and tomorrow, cultural and comfortable Catholics, or authentic and committed Catholics? The bishops in Vatican II agreed that it was time to return fully to the spirit of the Gospel and to preach that kind of Christianity to the nearly 4 billion persons in the world today, more than half of whom are under 25 years of age, and to the nearly 4 billion new persons who will be born into the world in the next 35 years.

This book, therefore, will attempt to balance the equation mentioned above. The equation can be stated more completely as the comparative worth of the schools in teaching Vatican II-defined Christianity vis-à-vis the difficulties of supporting schools which do so. We hope that this book will encourage bishops to opt for souls rather than statistics, and to move forward vigorously to implement Vatican II, and to let the chips fall where they may. They are men of Christian faith so they know that their obligation is to preach and practice authentic Christianity, not to shoehorn men into heaven.

I have more confidence in the fundamental good will and docility of the people in today's pews than the bishops seem to have. I am convinced that few, if any, people in the pews would leave the Church or reduce their support (generosity to a cause is the best sign of belief in it) because of the strong preachment of Christianity. It is more likely that, if true Christianity is not preached pretty soon, there will be no Christians in the pews in 35 years.

However this may be, there is a deeper reason for determining to teach authentic Christianity than the probability of its statistical success. Simply but starkly, it is what we are here for. To paraphrase the Gospel, "Teach all people all I have taught you and baptize those who accept me and my doctrine, even though the others may persecute you as they have me or may kill you as they will me." When men, including "our own," argue that it is imprudent or suicidal to preach and live whatever Christ commanded, and that it is, in effect, immoral to put mission ahead of survival, we must answer that the Gospels command otherwise.

Some say that a crisis of faith is the cause of all our confusions today. Faith is sometimes lost through reasoning because it seems to be incompatible with other sources of knowledge. But men may also lose faith secretly, even unconsciously, through rationalization, born of the difficulty and fear of living it. All of us who are the Church, from Pope to simple layman, should consider honestly the question whether today's crisis of faith in the Church and in ourselves may be caused by lack of courage rather than by lack of sophistication.

Hope is receiving great emphasis these days as the mark of the Christian rather than as a quality of the modern pagan. But hope without courage to do the things that make hope reasonable is superstition and presumption. Courage is today's most valuable virtue. Only with courage will we do what faith and charity command and thereby make hope justifiable.

The Purpose of Catholic Education

So much for the need to redefine the purpose of Catholic education and the manner in which redefinition should be undertaken. The remainder of this chapter will present some thoughts on what the purpose of Catholic education is. Foremost attention will be given to the worth of the schools as a means for performing the Church's teaching mission. Hopefully, we will conclude that the schools are indispensable to it and that their continued existence and development is justified in terms of basic need and value. Although some people say that the only justification for Catholic schools is that they happen to be there and that they provide, during a tolerable period of phase-out, busy-ness for otherwise idle hands and investment opportunities for otherwise idle dollars, we hope to show the pessimists a brighter and truer picture.

However, there is danger in claiming too much for the schools. They should not be regarded as the only means of providing Catholic education. There is a place at the present time for CCD work with both children and adults. It is a much more important place than is recognized, judging from the slender resources that are being devoted to it. There is a place for Catholic missions on secular college campuses, a place for parish study clubs, special formation groups, good sermons, a strong Catholic press and television.

Neither the schools, nor the other apostolates should be held responsible for accomplishing the Church's mission of developing committed Christians, but merely for performing their part of it. Our country's Constitution wisely protects only the right to pursue happiness; it does not guarantee its achievement. It is a mistake to hold the schools responsible for accomplishing the miracle of God's grace called Christian commitment, even though their precise *raison d'être* is to do all that is humanly possible in that behalf. Apparently this simple point cannot be emphasized enough in view of the judgments passed on the schools by certain intellectuals on the strength of the Greeley-Rossi and Notre Dame studies.

Those studies were extremely valuable and should be made continuously to check the results the schools are achieving, just as an important part of a business operation is the system it sets up to check results and to guide necessary changes to achieve better results. But any such study can be misinterpreted and even misused.

The Greeley-Rossi and Notre Dame studies are being misinterpreted by some to show that Catholic schools are hopeless as Catholic educational media. Too many self-styled experts are using them as proof that the schools should be abandoned, forgetting the fact mentioned earlier that they succeeded exceedingly well in imparting the pre-Vatican II kind of Catholic teaching. The studies proved that our schools do impart what they set out to teach. The common sense conclusion would seem to be: don't close the schools; change the thrust of their teaching.

But why Catholic schools at all? Why should we not relax and send our children to the public schools, and leave it to CCD teachers and CCD-educated parents to supply all that is needed to make them good Catholics?

The answer depends first upon what is meant by good Catholics.

If it means people who are born of Catholic parents and who are brought up in a Catholic community, who are Catholic, "of course," because they are of Italian or Irish or Spanish ancestry and who remain Catholic because of identification with that national or cultural background, that subcommunity in which they are comfortable, or of which they are proud, or which they see no practical reason for leaving, then there is no reason for Catholic schools. Parents can transmit that kind of cultural heritage, and CCD classes can supply a few rules and definitions to insure acquaintance with what is necessary to look like a good Catholic instead of a good Jew or a good Protestant. With public school-CCD methods we could probably generate down the years about as many adults content to call themselves Catholics as we now do.

But how do we develop in children a truly Catholic view of the great, astonishing, confusing world? How do we develop their ability to judge what is right or wrong about what they and other people are doing with the tremendously increasing and rapidly changing psychological, scientific and technological knowledge they are gaining? How do we show them that Catholicism not only is different from other religions and philosophies in its basic outlook on the world and man's place in it, but that this difference makes all the difference, and that Catholicism has a message for the world of the utmost importance in guiding the course of history? How do we motivate and aid children to participate in bringing that message to the world? How do we develop in them the positive conviction that all work is creative and that their own personal day-to-day work has worth and significance? How do we inculcate the negative conviction that their personal acts will be mischievous or even destructive unless those acts are of a kind and are performed in a way that is not only in accordance with God's will but also in accordance with the nature of this God-created world? How do we mend, through them, the world's schizophrenic split between body and soul, material and spiritual, secular and sacred, natural and supernatural—all of the things that Christ *integrated* once and forever? How do we convince them that this world is not just a vale of tears through which they are supposed to move painfully and cautiously on their way to another and better world, but that this world is also potentially that better world? If they and enough of their fellowmen learn how to act and do act as authentic human persons, persons who understand their nature as it was established by its Author, and live according to the human values revealed by that same Author through Jesus Christ, they can help create a better world. They already know that men can and eventually do achieve anything their value system indicates is significantly worthwhile.

How can we implement the theology of Catholic education described by Andrew Greeley in the opening section of this book and prepare our children to answer with enthusiasm and hope instead of boredom or despair the question that is consciously or subconsciously preoccupying an increasing number of people, young and old alike: "After affluence, what?"

Methods of Achieving the Purpose

There are two basic pedagogical methods. One is the deductive method by which facts, principles and wisdom developed by men from their observation and experience are applied to present-day hypothetical situations. The other method, the inductive, reasons from particulars to general principles using current situations. Both methods are and should be used in education. But both are subject to failure for the same reason, the inability of human beings to carry through, to relate principles and wisdom to applications on the one hand, and experience to principles and wisdom on the other hand. This is seen every day in the inability of adults to apply on Monday what they have been taught on Sunday and in their inability to learn from observation and experience. How long after Christ established His Church did it take for Christians to perceive that to enslave any man, black or white, is wrong? How long did men watch apples fall from trees before one of them formulated the principle of gravity? We are still debating the application of the principle of responsible parenthood. We are currently reexamining even the principle itself in the light of new knowledge derived from experience and observation.

Let us relate these remarks to Catholic education. It is both increasingly necessary and increasingly apparent that religious education and secular education should be integrated, that the relationship, the mutual relevance of the one to the other be deliberately and pointedly taught. Integration means the coordination, the concurrent mutual permeation, of secular and religious facts and principles. Pope John could be quoted on this point, but it is not his statement that makes it true. He said it because it is true. The world is secular. The same world is also sacred. Religious truths are not for the next world. They are for this world.

As a contemporary French writer once said, a man who lays a brick is helping to create the world. It is important for the world and for the salvation of the bricklayer's own soul that he know how to lay the brick well and that he perceive the religious as well as the secular significance of his laying the brick well. Men must also perceive the mutual relevance of religious truths and secular know-how to running a business, to creating and administering a social security system, an inner city development program or a foreign aid program, and to playing golf.

It is not useless to preach a sermon on Sunday. But it is an incomplete means of educating. It is not nonsense to urge parents to teach religious values to their children by word and by example, or for parents to follow that counsel. But again it is an incomplete form of education. It seldom touches more than simple moral situations. The values latent in the children's secular learning are not perceived by the children, and so they are not discussed with the parents. Even if children did discuss these problems, most parents are not equipped to provide the response needed. Not a hundred out of a million parents has enough secular knowledge for the mutual annotation process required, and only a handful are good teachers.

Some parents cannot teach their children even negative, though practical, rules of behavior so that the children become good enough to avoid jail or other social sanctions. Who would dare contend, in face of the history of mankind that parents can or will teach their children the positive virtues that make good citizens, neighbors, spouses and parents? These virtues are based upon religion and religious values, or they have no rational, dependable, motivating basis at all. Religion is a more and more complicated subject to teach, precisely because the day-to-day decisions it is supposed to guide are more and more complex. In today's world, the teaching of religion, involving the teaching of wisdom, values, reasons and applications is far more complicated than the teaching of English or philosophy. Yet no expert has ever advocated entrusting parents with teaching English or philosophy to their children, even in homes where excellent English is spoken and a wholesome philosophy is lived.

This is only one reason why the job of providing children with religious education need not and should not be left to parents. There is another practical reason. They simply will not do the job. This is not just a matter of bad will or laziness on their part. They know, as some of the experts apparently do not, that they cannot.

The intellectuals who are dissatisfied with current religious attitudes, especially within the Church itself, and who are doing so much to open up all the old questions, are often the very ones who say that we should phase out the schools and let the parents teach religion. They imply that religion is either a very simple subject or a useless one to teach, that it involves no serious questions, or that the questions may be asked but need not be answered in rational terms. They seem to hold that faith alone is necessary, and that faith does not require reasons or content.

Our Catholic schools may not have done a good job of teaching the mutual relevance of religion and secular subjects. Nevertheless, if Catholic schools did not exist, we would have to seriously consider establishing them. (At the very time we are talking of phasing out our schools for material reasons, many Jews and Protestants are establishing schools for religious reasons!) The interdependence of secular and religious knowledge points to a school that teaches both interdependently. The function of the modern Catholic school is to lead students to perceive the interdependence of the secular and the religious by pointing it out here and now, day-in-and-day-out. If Christianity is to be preserved as a life-giving force in the world, we must realize that there are no longer purely "secular subjects." Every subject is a religious secular subject and should be taught that way.

It does some good, but not enough, to establish a system by which children learn "secular subjects" in a public school five days a week and then "religion" in a one- or two-hour class on Saturday. We cannot expect by that method to relate the secular subjects to religion. Above all, we cannot overcome the idea that the two kinds of knowledge are separate and distinct and that the secular type is sufficient unto itself and sufficient unto them as it appears to be sufficient to their non-Catholic companions. Such a system is a compromise, and we should, if possible, avoid it in favor of the better one. It may result in forming good children. But holy children? Not if holy means whole, fully human, completely integrated persons, conscious of being a people commissioned by God to renew the face of the earth and prepared within the limits of their natural talents to do so.

Perhaps this opinion of the comparative value of the CCD kind of program is influenced too much by the widespread discouragement with its results. Perhaps more successful methods of keeping all of the children coming and of persuading more than one percent of the adults to attend classes or discussion groups for eighteen years so that they can properly instruct their children in the children's formative years, will be devised. It will always be more difficult to achieve integrated education by CCD methods, but in time reasonably satisfactory success in doing so may be achieved. Certainly we must try because it will be years before we can hope to provide schools for all our children.

We should not overlook the fact that, if the CCD system is to be successful, we must spend almost as much of our allegedly scarce resources of money and manpower as we would spend for a system of properly located schools. We will have to provide almost as many classrooms. We will have to recruit almost as many teachers of the same professional competence. And a large number of these teachers will have to be permanently dedicated to the work and will have to be paid competitive salaries. In a word, if we decide to use the public schools plus CCD, we should realize that this choice will not greatly relieve the resources and money problems. This will be apparent when we really start to implement and extend CCD programs as we should. We can conclude from these reflections that we should continue to improve and expand our school system unless and until CCD programs prove to be the better way from both the educational and the resources standpoints.

Considering what has been said to this point about the purpose of Catholic education, it seems highly unlikely that CCD programs will ever be able to do the job the schools can do. Only in the Catholic schools can total knowledge be taught or learned today. They are the answer to the uneasiness of the young who believe that they are being shortchanged in secular schools and colleges. We should gain confidence that our schools and colleges are *the* place to educate the young and that we need only intelligent and courageous implementation to make them the leading educational enterprise of the day. It is an incredible time to be talking about phasing them out.

The Role of Parents

Ruling out a role for parents in the formal religious education of their children does not mean that parents have no part at all to play in the religious education of the children. They have just as important a part to play as the schools. We will discuss the parents' role in this chapter and in Chapter 4 we will discuss how they may be prepared to perform it.

A professional psychologist or sociologist might describe his outstanding function and contribution to be to verify by research, and then to put into precise terminology, truths which he has first suspected with the insights of common sense. These specialists say that many of the "difficult," sometimes rebellious, members of the younger generation bear all of the earmarks of rejected children. A "rejected child" is a child without healthy self-esteem because his parents—sometimes really and consciously, often only apparently or subconsciously—did not love him. If these children are rejected children, their future is dim insofar as their ability to acquire sufficient self-esteem to achieve internal peace and satisfactory relationships to others is concerned. Their feeling of rejection may also account for their pathetic desire to be loved, for the tragedy of their inability to trust others enough to love them or to trust truth enough to commit themselves to it.

Psychologists, sociologists and socio-psychologists are also pointing out that human beings are formed in their most important drives, outlooks on life, and problem-solving or decision-making attitudes by the experiences of the first few—normally not more than five or six—years of their lives. So, parents bear responsibility for their children's character formation and children are victims for life of their parents' attitude toward their environment. Environment extends to the community outside the home as well as within the home. Overcoming the handicap of a bad formation in these early years is possible but difficult, particularly if the child resists change.

A third fact of which the psychologists and sociologists are reminding us is something we should all remember from our own experience, namely, that from the time children enter their teens they are influenced by their friends and associates as much as and sometimes more than by their parents. Add to this the fact that children spend more time outside the home, and that even in the home they are exposed to strong outside influences through that new educating medium, television. The possibility that parents can be broadly effective educators is shrinking.

All this suggests that parents should be providing their children, not education in formal secular or religious subjects, but love and sane, healthy attitudes. Their role in the education of their children is not only of crucial and fundamental importance; it is also a supremely difficult full-time job. Just learning how to communicate their love of their children without being weakly sentimental or permissive, learning how to teach the younger children wonder and prayerfulness, and the older ones (at the right stage of their development, but especially not prematurely) responsibility and respect, should occupy much time spent attending lectures, studying, discussing and reading. And guiding the children in the application of what is learned requires, ideally, personal presence and attention of the parents during all of the waking hours of the children. The ideal cannot, of course, be met because at least one parent per family must hold an outside job.

At any rate, it is plain that in a normal household there is little time for a parent to give any amount of formal education to the children. But this should not concern them because, if they communicate love, cheerfulness and peace, the children's formal education in any subject, including religion, can safely be left to others. If parents fail to provide their children with these qualities, the children, and the adult society which they will soon become, will be seriously disadvantaged no matter how educated they become, or how they become educated.

Some people may think that I advocate that parents teach and apply a suspiciously natural type of religion to their children. This is precisely the kind of religion parents should impart to their children to help them develop into Christians. Without the natural foundations described, there is little likelihood that true and sturdy Christians will develop. Even when we remember that grace builds on nature, we often fail to realize that without a sound natural foundation grace has little upon which to build. No one works his way to holiness, even with the necessary help of God, except through his own efforts to perfect himself in the natural virtues. It is the natural virtues of prudence, temperance, fortitude and justice that support at the outset and from day to day the increase of faith, hope and charity we pray for. In providing this natural foundation, the parents will, of course, act out of religious motives and will instill the same motives in their children. To sum up, they will provide the children with an integrated religious-natural training in the virtues.

Parents should eschew the formal teaching of religion, therefore, just as they do the teaching of the new math. Instead they should form and maintain the children's basic attitude of willingness to learn, to be open to the new math and to religion and to support the teaching of both by praising the children's accomplishments. Incidentally, parents who listen to their children as they should are likely to pick up a few valuable bits of learning for the good of their own morals and souls. The schools and children have always played this indirect role in the education of adults, a valuable fallout, too seldom appreciated in assessing the value of schools and children.

4. The Development of Programs

There has seldom, if ever, been a more exciting and challenging time for designing and carrying out Catholic educational programs. Just how do we implement the theological principles and new directions suggested in the opening essay in this book and the general purpose and particular goals outlined in Chapter 3. Both aspects of Catholic education—what to teach and how to teach it—present new and staggering problems. There is no need to document that statement more extensively than Father Andrew Greeley does in his contribution to this book. It is not necessary to trace the historical developments that have brought us to this point. It is futile to wring our hands about it and cowardly to retire from the scene. We must face the present with faith and courage, and we must work for the future with hope and confidence. We must meet the challenges because we love ourselves, our children and our fellowmen, and because the challenges have been presented by God Himself at this stage of His salvation history.

Factors That Make Catholic Education a New Ball Game

In our day, God has further revealed Himself to men and in the process has further revealed men to themselves. Significantly, one of the revelations is about revelation itself. It is a new thing for Catholics to realize that God reveals Himself throughout history—not just once on Mount Sinai and once again on Mount Calvary, but always and forever in, through and by the world, especially the world of men. We used to think we had a pretty good grip on God, Christ and his Church. Our certainties about them were well developed long before we began to classify and catalog certainties about the stars and atoms. The very attitude of confidence we had in our ability to classify and define the divine mysteries provided the foundation of our confidence that we could do the same about the mysteries of the universe. It is not strange, then, that our certainties should be jolted simultaneously in both fields of knowledge.

We have suddenly learned that all we can say about the reality of anything is: "This is the way it looks to us now. This is the truth as we see it now about God, about man, about atoms and stars, about energy, about life and about the meaning of human life. This is enough to know to live in reasonable peace and comfort with ourselves and our neighbors today. We will continue to try to learn more, to proceed from this truth to fuller truth so that we may live tomorrow in greater peace and comfort with ourselves and our neighbors."

Not until the Second Vatican Council did the Church join the modern world in its recognition that for every truth there is fuller truth. It is painfully apparent that adjustment to the idea that the Church is a pilgrim like the rest of mankind is coming hard. Movement is difficult from the position that "This is the truth" to the position that "This is the truth as we see it today." Many of us still say "Lord, I believe exactly this; help me to believe it that way." We have not yet humbly bowed before the limitless, transcendent God and said: "Lord, I believe exactly this; help me to correct it in due time if it is in any way incorrect or incomplete."

The Church along with science has learned that truth is a strange thing. It is not really a thing at all. It is only a relationship between a real thing and our idea of it. Real things are real; they are exactly what they are. Truth, however, is a work of the mind. It is the mind's accurate grasp or understanding of what the real thing really is. If the mind's understanding is inaccurate or incomplete, truth about the thing does not exist. Only some truth, or relative truth, about it exists.

Man's drive to ascertain truth has been insatiable. Man has been defined as the animal who seeks truth. He has used what he has learned to make a better world—too often for number one man at the expense of others, but nevertheless a better world from that limited and selfish point of view. The area of darkness he has explored most persistently has been himself: "Who am I? From whence did I come? Why am I here? Where am I going? What should I do to get there? Is it worthwhile? Does it make sense?"

True answers to those questions have always struck men as being vastly more important than true answers about the nature of stones or trees or cattle. At the same time, evidence upon which to base answers has been far more difficult to find, and techniques for finding and observing the evidence have been far more difficult to devise. Yet some answers had to be found to satisfy man that human life was worthwhile and not absurd. He has in every age and every culture seized upon answers given by men such as Gautama Siddartha, Moses, Mohammed and Jesus Christ who said that God had revealed the answers to them. Men studied the answers very carefully, reduced them to laws ensuring salvation, found all possible loopholes, resisted the spirit of the laws and enforced the letter.

In olden times, prophets and savants who challenged any part of the resulting system were called heretics or enemies of society, and they were stoned to death, or thrown to the lions or burned at the stake unless they recanted. Today such men are called disrupters, or disobedient or disloyal, and they are maligned, ostracized or ignored.

We are a Church which has defined many truths, not in terms of, "This is the way it looks to us today." This would have been quite sufficient to guide contemporary men. Instead we defined truth dogmatically with a flat, "This is the way it is, period." One truth so defined was that the Church was acting under the guidance and authority of God himself when defining truth, and hence that a proposition defined by it was indeed the full truth of the matter, period. When such a Church redefines such a definition, it understandably unsettles many people. Yet, under the guidance of the Holy Spirit and the modern perceptiveness of the bishops, it has done so, despite its temporary unsettling effect. The Church has not changed its mind about the reality of revelation. It has simply broadened its notion of how revelation takes place, and it has given recognition to a few facts about truth.

It has been demonstrated that in men's attempt to learn what even material things really are—material objects that can be clamped down and then taken apart with the utmost care and measured and weighed with the utmost precision—complete success is never achieved because the thing is changed by the very process of dissection and measurement. Only partial or relative truth about it can be obtained.

Men have studied themselves and each other as individuals and as groups or societies for the same purpose—to learn the truth about themselves and each other. This is considerably more difficult because it requires constant effort to devise better tools of observation and also because the phenomenon of the subject's changing while or because of the process of observation may occur in human subjects as well as in material subjects.

Men also realize now that in both the physical and the human sciences it is likely that error may lie in the eye of the observer or in the mental processes he must use to interpret his observations. For that reason the same individual, or preferably different groups of individuals, may make repeated observations of the same subject. Even so, blind spots and biases of the observers tend to color, not only interpretations of the data, but even the accuracy of the observations which the data record, especially in the human sciences.

Science has learned to live with such relative truths. It works patiently to narrow the margins of error, but no scientist seems to believe that at some time in the future all possibility of error in observation or interpretation will be eliminated. No man of common sense is disturbed about this situation, since even relative truth is sufficient for the ends of any science, that is, to advance the frontiers of knowledge and to use this knowledge for better health, greater comfort, more gracious living. It is almost as though science said: "Nature, or Providence, or God or Someone will take care of men well enough despite the ignorance of men, just as he takes care of the lilies of the field!"

A pity men have not been similarly relaxed about religious truths. No man has seen God. Everything we know about him has been pried out by men from the stuff of creation. Each of us makes his own observations and interpretations, but we rely chiefly upon the recorded observations and interpretations of other men who preceded us down the ages. The significant event upon which Christianity itself is based we know from the writings of men who were recording their own observations, or the accounts of eyewitnesses and their interpretations of those observations. We believe what they believed because they believed it. One element of their belief was that the grace of God was necessary to their belief. We believe that, too, because we are rational men who would otherwise consider the essential story wholly incredible.

We have developed a vast set of religious truths from that slender record. Well and good. It is all we have to go by. But we have come at long last to admit that some of the interpretations of the meaning of the original writers may not have been completely accurate. We concede that those interpretations may have been correct for the interpreters. We concede that partly because we are forced to admit that we are not sure what the interpretations meant even to the interpreters. So we merely say that their interpretations, though valuable, are not sufficient for us, and we return to the original writers and make our own reassessments. In doing this we carefully consider the intervening interpretations in the light of their historical context, and we modify them only to the extent demanded by new sources of information and better tools of research and interpretation. Among other things that we notice is that the original writers were remarkably relaxed about the significance of things which later generations fretted about to the point of killing each other when they disagreed over what the writers meant. At the same time we downgrade the interpreters not because of their excessive zeal, but only when and to the extent we believe they were wrong.

Quite obviously, this shift in outlook toward truth is of great importance to Catholic education. It will affect secular education, too, and secular educators who were brought up in the old school of certainties about the world and man have not yet adjusted to the changes. Catholic educators have a double task, two fields to deal with in which certainty has passed to relative certainty. The nature of the required mental adjustment and the attendant difficulty of making it are much the same in each case. But in practice it will be found more difficult to make the adjustment in the case of religious truth.

Yet it opens the windows of the Church to the world and the

windows of the world to the Church. It leads to a vast exploration of the significance of Christ as man, and of the Church as the sacrament of Christ present as the visible sign of the unity of men in Christ. It gives the Church relevance to the world and to the secular city. It gives the Church credibility when it addresses the world and the secular city. It restores the Church to its position as a leader of all men in its God-given task of shaping and perfecting the world. To be effective, a leader must understand and speak meaningfully to the questions and problems of his followers. The change in the Church's attitude toward truth will enable it to speak to the questions and problems of the men of the world. The Church will be concerned not only with doctrinal or moral questions but with all problems as the men of the world see them, and hence as they really are. From now on the Church will be constantly studying all sources of truth and developing additional and sometimes different answers.

The first thing Catholic educators must teach these days is this new understanding of truth. Even the catechism format of religion textbook can be used as an educational aid if teachers use it with the proper open attitude. No one would think it sensible to junk all of today's physics and chemistry textbooks and teach physics and chemistry with clippings from the daily newspaper just because knowledge about energy and the composition of matter is likely to change tomorrow. Textbooks in every secular subject, however, have changed about every five years in the last twenty-five years because of the knowledge explosion. No one's life has been shattered because of it. Until completely upsetting new knowledge is gained, old knowledge has been found to be of great practical use, as well as sufficient to provide a position from which to move to greater knowledge.

In fact, until new knowledge has been subjected to every conceivable test and check, and found really to upset old knowledge, science retains, uses and teaches the old knowledge. The Church will do the same. Catholic educators will still teach about the transcendent God and about the reality and destructive evil of sin. They will continue to teach that God's Son became authentic man; that men crucified him because of His teachings; that he was raised from the dead and thus conquered the ultimate evil of sin. They will relate what he told us about himself, ourselves, and our brothers, about God, his Father and ours, and why the Church believes those things. Catholic educators will continue to clarify the helpful and hopeful implications of all these truths for us and for our fellow men, now and forever. They will be the same old truths, but teachers will present them as the Church sees them *now* with openness to the possibility and the hope that the Church may see them more clearly tomorrow, if all of the people who are the Church keep working at it as they should.

"The people who are the Church." There is hope and peril in that term. There is hope if those who are the Church continue on the course laid out by Vatican II, peril if they do not. The Church described by the bishops in the Second Vatican Council can be taught to modern men, including our children with confidence and self-respect. There is no other Church worth teaching. If our educational programs are not geared to carry on the Church of Vatican II, they will not deserve our support.

What if that Church does not quickly appear? What if the old, closed Church seems to prevail? That Church by its manner of acting too often appears to violate its God-given nature and renders incredible its claim to be Christ present in the world. Such a Church cannot be preached to modern men, including our children, with any hope of success. Such a Church cannot be the leader of mankind to peace, sanity, community. What then?

Then we will hold on to our Christian faith by the skin of our teeth. We will learn to live with tension and ambiguity. We will fight injustices and work for structures to ensure justice. We will modify the Church's claim to be the custodian of all religious truth to a modest assertion that it is an honest broker of religious truth. We will purify ourselves and preach the pure Church to others. Unless we do this, men of less faith will obstruct Christ's will for his Church. A pilgrim Church requires a tougher, more adult faith than one in which everything is settled and certain. If we truly love God and His world, we will not become cop-outs from his Church, and we will not abandon His Church to cop-outs from Christianity.

The Generation Gap, Knowledge Gap and Credibility Gap

My purpose in this section of the book is to present the real experts and the rank and file of the teaching community with sufficient questions and challenges to get them to rethink why they are teaching at all. In the light of their answers, they should decide what to teach and how to teach it to be effective, particularly with today's children and young people and with the even greater number of new persons who will be born and proceed through the schools in the next generation. Half of the people in our country today are under 26. About 25 million of them are Catholic children and young people. About 6 million young people—a fourth of them Catholic—reach adulthood every year!

The term "program" as used in this section includes both content or curriculum and method or means. These two essential parts of an educational program could no doubt be discussed separately, a book to each. Let the experts write the books. We will treat the parts together from the point of view that content dictates method, and that method should enhance content and not destroy it.

We have the same problem and use much the same approach in discussing "man." We treat separately his body or material needs and his soul or spiritual needs. Yet we know he is a body-soul and that we had better not mentally or verbally dissect him so completely that he becomes dehumanized.

We mention "man" here not only to illustrate the point about the content-method unity of program, but also to emphasize that it is men that we are trying to educate. Our difficulties in doing so seem to stem largely from the fixed idea that today's man is the same as yesterday's man. He is not.

Nothing will be gained for our purposes to argue whether human nature has changed over the centuries, much less in the last twenty years. The plain and only fact that should interest educators is that educable man has changed and is still changing. We call this phenomenon "the generation gap." We know very well to the point of dismay and frustration that it is a very real thing. We used to say that the spread between generations was about twenty-five years. Teachers say it is now four or five years.

Obviously, the biological gap has not narrowed. But just as obviously the knowledge gap and the psychological gap have. What the present generation knows at fourteen equals in facts what previous generations knew at forty. What the present generation needs to know is different and more extensive than the previous generation needed to know. Finally, what the present generation thinks it is important to know and its attitude toward learning are different—distressingly different in the opinion of adults educated in earlier times and now trying, in annoyance and frustration, to pass on their wisdom in the same way they acquired it.

The changed attitude about what is important to know is the crux of the generation gap. It affects all adult-child relationships, including the formal education programs of the schools and colleges. In schools and colleges, at least, the generation gap is a compound of the knowledge gap and the credibility gap.

The generation gap baffles young people. Children and adolescents have never been particularly adept at analyzing and solving their own problems. Adults are stupid to expect them to do so now. We adults should stop blaming the young for their problems, and we should stop cursing them for not "shaping up." We should assume our adult responsibilities to the young and admit to ourselves that their problems are not, fundamentally, of their creation but of ours.

The adult world which young people are being propelled into is a world of our own hang-ups and frustrations about our world. If it is a good world, we should be able to persuade our children that it is good. If it is not so good, we should do our best to change it so that it will be fit for our children to enter. How can we blithely say, "Let future generations take care of themselves?" "Future generations" is an abstract term we use when we uneasily try to obscure from ourselves the fact that "future generations" means precisely our children and our grandchildren or those of our closest relatives or dearest friends. As responsible adults, we are the ones who should "shape up." We should be doing today what we can to make a better world. We should be providing our children with the equipment to live in the almost unimaginably more populous and complex world they will inherit from us in a few years.

So, in devising and conducting educational programs, we must provide factual knowledge in keeping with the times. But since the knowledge explosion has made it impossible to present, much less to learn, more than a limited amount of facts, and since factual knowledge continues to expand and even to change, we must teach students how to learn. Since learning is difficult and one of the biggest difficulties these days seems to be lack of motivation, we must teach them why knowledge should be pursued all one's life.

In other terms, we must supply students a systematic input of facts in the academic disciplines, guide them in the assimilation and integration of these and all other facts and lead them to an intense desire for wisdom, the fullness of learning. Guidance and leadership are giant steps beyond the usual concept of education. They add "selling" to "telling," and "here's how to use it" to "here it is."

In meeting the last requirement we will run into the "credibility gap." The knowledge gap can be filled mechanically by teaching facts and skills for learning facts. But if students believe that their instructors are trying to fit them into and thus perpetuate a world of systems, institutions and practices which the students abhor or fear, they will resist the teaching and refuse to learn. They will consider such teaching useless at best, threatening or demonic at worst.

The great challenge to educators these days is to present to all, not just to the young, the possibility of a world which meets the aspirations of mankind. They are challenged to hold out the hope that realization of that world is possible and to furnish the know-how for leveraging the change. The problem, of course, is whether people who teach within the present system can successfully do all that. This is the problem of the credibility gap.

It is a problem as old as mankind. The young have always pushed for a better world than the one their elders were apparently content with. Change for the better has come about in those eras when adults retained their youthful idealism and determination. Progress has slackened or failed when the young became contented or apathetic as they grew older. The quality of leadership among the adults of the age had more to do with progress or decline than the idealism or cynicism of the young. In the great battles for social progress, the generals have been adults, leading volunteer armies of the young. Without adult understanding and guidance, the answers and solutions proposed by the young could be as unrealistic or demonic as the situations they dislike or fear.

Our day presents a unique opportunity to the Church which has God's mandate to help fashion a better world for men and to renew the face of the earth until it is fit for the return of its Redeemer. It is a time for the Church to move forward vigorously with the vision and guidance the world so badly needs. But the credibility gap is felt in the Church, too. Will the Church in our day provide the kind of leaders who will inspire followers? It will if the Church practices what it preaches and thus escapes the charge of hypocrisy hurled by the young at many of the other institutions of society.

Different Programs for Different Groups

Let us try to bring these general remarks into useful focus.

Programs must necessarily be based upon and designed to implement the purposes of education. We have seen that the purpose of all Catholic education from generation to generation until the end of time is to teach the truths of the Catholic faith, authentic Christianity, and the relevance and importance of those truths to all aspects and activities of life to the end that every person in the Catholic community may achieve holiness and wholeness, and thus think and act fruitfully with love for themselves, for each other and for their neighbors in the larger community.

The Catholic community is itself large and diverse. We will divide it, for educational purposes, into seven groups: 1. Catholic children attending Catholic grade schools; 2. Catholic children attending Catholic high schools; 3. Catholic children attending public grade and high schools; 4. Catholic young people attending Catholic colleges and universities; 5. Catholic young people attending other colleges and universities; 6. Catholic adults; 7. Catholic children and adults who are disadvantaged.

Different means and methods of transmitting truth and gaining commitment to it are necessary to reach persons who differ in maturity, experience and place in society. Children require one approach, young people another, adults still another. What is relevant to children of the well-to-do and the advantaged means little to children of the poor and the disadvantaged. The religious situation of children in public schools differs radically from that of children in Catholic schools.

Effective programming is the product of experience with methods which work best to achieve the educational results desired. Hence, the most important thing about programs is that every program should be regarded as more or less experimental and subject to continual replanning on the basis of results achieved, and better or new goals to be sought.

Educational systems are not notable for their acceptance of that principle. And, of course, the principle is difficult to effectuate. It calls for careful appraisal of the characteristics and needs of each particular group, the establishment of goals to meet the needs in view of those characteristics and the assignment of appropriate resources, especially personnel having the right qualifications, to meet the goals. Measures must be devised to check the successes and shortcomings of each program on an on-going basis. Performance of the planning and organizing steps requires special professional competence. These functions should be performed by a central administrative and resource staff, such as a diocesan office of education, in close cooperation with those conducting each program (parish school principals, CCD directors, heads of experimental programs), and in open communication with those benefiting from the programs (students, parents, the public). In institutions of higher learning, the task of planning, consulting, organizing and checking falls upon the administration of the institution.

Hence, there will be several programs. Resources will be affected, for different teaching talents and facilities will be needed for each type of program. The structure for each program will differ, and at the same time some form of overall structure must exist to coordinate and provide services to all of the individual programs. Directors will have to determine costs for each program to determine whether all programs can be suitably and adequately provided for, or whether they must be modified, or priorities established, if revenues are inadequate.

The structure problem will be treated in Chapter 5, the money problem in Chapter 6. In the remainder of this chapter we will discuss educational programs to meet the needs of the seven groups listed above. We will try to explore their relative importance to provide a basis for setting priorities in case revenues turn out to be insufficient.

Catholic Grade Schools

Many people, including some experts in educational matters, say that if we must reduce our educational venture because of insufficient resources, the grade schools should be the place to start, beginning with grades one and two. This seems to make sense for two reasons: first, children are formed in their basic attitudes toward religion and toward learning during their preschool years; and second, children of grade school age are not yet sufficiently reasoning creatures to benefit significantly from intellectual permeation or penetration of the secular with the religious in teaching.

On the other hand, children of this age are still in their formative years; they are still learning at a more rapid rate than they ever will again. The question of what they should be taught at this age is, therefore, just as important as it is at other ages.

Intellectual integration of the secular and the religious is one thing. Emotional and moral integration are equally important. We can laugh all we will at Christmas plays, daily Mass in an aroma of candles and incense, and arithmetic based on numbers of saints and angels, but they do make lasting impressions on mind and soul. Better methods of teaching religion through the senses and emotions are desirable and should be used these days. There is no point, for instance, in taking a chance that a child's natural aversion to memorizing the multiplication tables might be transferred to the saints and angels. But there is no effective substitute for associating the religious with the child's enjoyment of color, music, flowers and incense. The deepest, most memorable experiences of our lives are associated with such aesthetic pleasures.

The alternative is to relegate the children to a school which is religiously and morally neutral and hence sterile of natural supports to the religious and moral development of the child. In such schools even the secular celebration of Christmas in terms of Santa Claus is often excluded, and the example of folk heroes is the only reason for morality children are likely to hear.

Children are not struggling for identity as teen-agers are. But they are getting it. By the time they are teen-agers, they will have an identity, although it may suddenly become confused or unsatisfactory. Attendance at a Catholic grade school provides children painlessly and happily with identity as Catholics and as members of the Catholic community. It is not the identity of a very mature Catholic, and it will no doubt be rethought and have to be regained, but at least it will have been acquired. That is no small value. It will assume a greater value as we learn more about kerygmatic methods of teaching religion and the use of the arts and child-level liturgical forms. As a very practical matter, it prepares a child to move easily into a Catholic high school. There is no trauma of separation from friends at that point; there is no resistance to what is taught there.

Methods of teaching religion to children are improving especially for the preteen years when the children are receiving the sacraments for the first time. They are being better prepared for those joyful events than were their parents. Stress is on God's love of us and our love of God and neighbor, not upon sin and fear of punishment. First confession is often deferred until the child is ten or twelve years of age. Each grade or class has its day of the week when it celebrates the Eucharist within the sanctuary gathered around the priest. The next Greeley-Rossi research project should show that the new content and method of teaching religion is achieving more genuinely Christian formation than the old.

The catechism has not been relegated to the scrap heap, any more than have the alphabet, the spelling book or the rules of the new math. Even though the new math cannot be fully comprehended now, or perhaps ever, the rules are still memorized. The rules can be very useful equipment whether they are understood or not. The basic truths of the Catholic faith should be taught and memorized to provide a basis for reflection all one's life. To be sure, they should be explained more than they were explained to the present generation of adults, and they should be explained in terms appropriate to a child's level of understanding and experience. They will be part of the child's equipment for developing greater understanding as questions occur to him, or are put to him, later. The child may then remember the answers, only partly understood now. Perhaps more importantly, he will remember that there are answers.

More has been learned and is being applied in the schools about children's need for individual love and attention. We have earlier noted the tragic fact that many children suffer from lack of love from their parents, or failure of their parents to communicate their love effectively. This destroys the child, if the lack is not somehow compensated. The Catholic schools should be particularly able to supply love and attention and happily make up for what may be lacking in the home. Teachers should be qualified to be strong and loving mother and father figures to the children. They are not limited, as they would be in the public schools. They can show that love reaches across the whole breadth of the child's needs and into the very depths of his soul. The school should reach out to the parents individually with suggestions and guidance to help them provide Christian home atmosphere, a basically human atmosphere, which is indispensable to the formation of authentic human beings.

Finally, we must say what should be needless to say. Our grade schools must teach well all secular subjects which are recognized as important today. National tests show that most of our schools teach what they undertake to teach as well as most of the public schools do. But the most often heard reasons for parents' transferring their children from their parish school to their neighboring public school are: their parish school is not as good generally as their public school; or—more often—their parish school does not teach some important subject, such as science, or that it has no special programs to assist slow learners or children with speech defects. We must have schools with courses as reasonably comprehensive and effective as those of the public schools, and we must have schools of uniform excellence.

Catholic High Schools

Adolescents are suddenly aware of the outside world. At the same time it is the age of confusion and uncertainty about one's self. Identity must be reacquired or reformed in the light of a completely new awareness of self, often an awareness of a seemingly new self. It is the age of dreams and daydreams, of exhilarating idealism and depressing disenchantment, of high enthusiasm and deep discouragement, all in bewildering and unaccountable mixtures and sudden swings. Sexual development makes its sudden transforming appearance and is rapidly completed. The children are biologically men and women long before they are psychologically adjusted to understand and cope with the change. Their reactions to it range from insatiable curiosity to inexpressible terror. The stresses and strains of becoming authentically human—physically, mentally, and emotionally—are at their peak.

Lucky the child who has parents who not only remember their own adolescence but who also have learned how to support the child through these turbulent years of transition to adulthood. There is no hard evidence that many of today's children are favored in that respect. On the contrary. Although today's children are subject to even greater stress than their parents were, most of today's parents seem singularly unprepared to help them. Both parents and children need the benefit of professional counseling in what has been learned about adolescents. Few parents can be reached that way, but the children can be reached because they are in the schools.

High school teachers must, of course, be qualified to teach secular subjects as well as they are taught in the public schools. In addition, they must present strong community figures, not authoritarian but authentic, capable of guiding the students into readiness for friendship.

It is a truism that the purpose of the education of children is to prepare them to be adults through the stages of developing skills and achieving satisfying relationships with other people. As Catholics, we would hasten to amplify that statement by interjecting "authentic" adults. "Authentic" here, as elsewhere in this book, is used in its root meaning of "as coming from, or as designed by, its author or creator." An adolescent child is in the final stages of that development, the stage in which the process is at its rapidly resolving climax. Teachers of adolescents must be prepared to deal with them as children one day, adults the next day and somewhere in between at any time.

The chances are that the problems of bringing adolescents out of their recessive moods and lifting them another step toward adulthood will be less difficult than the problems of holding them down and persuading them to be patient with themselves and docile toward teaching for just a few more years. Teaching programs which incorporate action projects have two values: they help the students to progress toward adult responsibilities and competence, and they demonstrate to the students that they still have much to learn.

At this age students benefit most from strong integration of the religious and the secular. The teacher of every secular subject (with some possible exceptions, like mathematics and foreign languages— though not foreign language literature) will permeate the subject with religious values, observations and insights. There will be strong religion courses (probably required but not credit) which teach, not only the basic catechism truths, but also permit students to discuss every aspect of life as they experience it. Points of view are explained, criticized or applauded in the light of Christian truths and values. This student participation will help them to understand who they are—themselves, personally—and what their worth is. This is the most important lesson they will ever learn.

Integrating should be done on such an immediate and all-embracing scale and with such an open attitude that the students are convinced that every type of human activity and problem has a religious aspect, and should and can be shaped or solved by intelligent and goodwill application of Christian principles and secular knowledge and skill. They will emerge with the wholesome attitude that the world is not an obstacle course of pitfalls and traps designed by a mean and vengeful Being to hurt, possibly to damn them. Instead, they will be sure that the world is truly the seed ground of glory, and that if it is used in ways that accord with their own nature, it will be good, rational, perfectible and enjoyable. Their questions about pain and suffering, injustice and evil, which they will learn about in the course of their studies of secular subjects and which they will experience or observe in their own lives, will be answered then and there in Christian terms—all the Church knows about them today, and all she will learn about them tomorrow.

It is difficult to understand the criticism some teachers level at on-the-spot integration of the secular and the religious. They say, for instance, that English literature is English literature and not Catholic English literature. They insist that only the facts and principles of physiology and economics should be studied and that no Catholic value judgments should be made on what these facts and principles show about people or the institutions and practices they describe. They say that history should not be taught as a course in Church history apologetics.

One can agree with those statements and yet insist that a teacher who phrases them that way and actually teaches literature, physiology, economics or history without reference to religious values, insights and positions is not teaching the subject well because he is not teaching it completely. So he is unjust to both the subject and the students. Why are children being taught at all if not to help them understand themselves and to make correct decisions in the present and sound plans for the future? Is not fleshless, ivory tower teaching exactly what college students—and, more and more, high school students—claim is short-changing them today?

Criticisms of integrated teaching, often accompanied by accusations of brainwashing, make it seem as though the critics are saying that they see no relevance of religion, especially Catholicism, to anything, or that it is somehow unfair and underhanded to help children to perceive the relevance. The same can be said about a teacher of religion who fails to mention the insights supplied by literature, history, economics and sociology to religious problems and questions. Both must be wrong. Children cannot cope with amorality in ideas any more than they can cope with immorality in example. A school established for the purpose of forming children to be mature Catholics and of teaching the relevance of Catholic truths to all learning and experience should confront every point of view expressed in literature, every tenet of philosophical systems, every description of human beings and human institutions and social customs, every historical twist and turn of man with positive Catholic criticism. If the Church is what she claims to be, she has the right and obligation to pass judgment on the past actions and thoughts of men as well as on present and future ones precisely for the sake of the present and the future.

I do not contend here—and, since Vatican II, there is less and less danger that it will be successfully contended elsewhere—that the Church has all the answers. But she has the Gospels and a unique view of truth and truthfulness to use in arriving at the answers. If she will be true to herself and her mission, she will be the light of the world. Knowledge is power. Christian wisdom is superpower. It is the way, the truth, and the life, and it is energized by love, the kind of love that is not domineering or paternalistic, but humble and educative in the radical sense of both terms.

Another objection to the deliberate and overt integration or permeation method of teaching is presented by some educators who hold that children gain all they need to know about goodness and values from teachers who have both. They say that such teachers somehow communicate goodness and values, nonverbally, simply by being there. These educators point to the apparent fact that children in public schools gain moral strength and values from their teachers even though the teachers are forbidden to teach religious truths. It is quite certain that the values of the current culture are transmitted that way. This is what many people, especially those whose skin is black, object to about most schools, including religious ones, these days. But, if the schools are to be used, as they should be, to change or motivate a value system, teachers must not only hold and live the values they wish to transmit to the children but they must also communicate them with more than personal presence. They must use the power of the word. It is impossible to imagine that Christianity would have even been born, much less that it would exist today, if Jesus Christ had taught his disciples a straight course in Assyrian history or a straight course in the beauty of the Jewish scriptures as literature.

Another interesting debate is being conducted these days about a new theory of what and how children should be taught. Some educators have broken loose from existing structures in order to put the theory to work. Others, including several of the teaching orders of brothers and sisters who have never belonged to a structured school system are trying out the theory—that it is far better to teach how to learn facts, how to judge their relative importance and their relationships and how to put them to use for the true benefit of men than it is merely to teach facts. Basic facts in all the recognized academic disciplines are taught, but since it would be impossible, because of the knowledge explosion, to teach all the facts in each discipline, a careful selection is made, and the students are taught how to get the rest of the facts and tomorrow's facts out of books as well as by simply but carefully observing things and events. However, the real emphasis is not upon the piling up of facts but rather upon the showing of principles and relationships. Team teaching has been found to be an effective way to do this.

Students take examinations in all academic subjects but emphasis is not on what facts they learned but on whether they learned how to learn facts. Facts come into the picture, of course, but chiefly to enable the student to give meaningful answers to the examination questions. These are thought questions designed to test reasoning more than memory. Marks or grades, if given at all, are given as much to guide the teacher with respect to the effectiveness of his teaching as to indicate to the student his achievement. Credit, passing, is a matter of the professional judgment of the teacher in consultation with the student. This is similar to the modern business management technique of periodic performance reviews to let the employee know how he is doing and to provide a reasonably objective basis for determining his readiness for advancement.

This method of educating may not generate ecstasy, as some enthusiasts say education should. But it does hold promise of generating interest rather than boredom and of producing more self-reliant, resourceful and better adjusted young men and women. Students so trained should be able to remain masters of themselves and of the machines they operate or create.

This kind of education requires teachers who not only know their academic disciplines but who are integrated persons, and ones who are available for consultation. Moving pictures, slides, audio-visual tapes and closed-circuit television are used for the more effective and economical presentation of facts to large groups of students. But the real teaching is done in groups where dialogue between students and teacher is the chief tool used. Students are at all times encouraged to raise questions, and never turned off when they do.

The Catholic high school is designed to guide and assist children through the restless years of adolescence from the simplicities of childhood to the threshold of adulthood so that they may emerge with commitment to the proposition that their religion is the most important part of the beings they have become. The school's goal is to drive into the being of every child the living conviction that he is a child of God, that God is a loving Father who knows the child better than the child himself does, that the personal and social values he revealed in and through Jesus Christ are natural to the child, and that their observance is the only guarantor of the child's happiness here as well as hereafter. If the school's program is successful, the children will have been given a position from which to judge sanely and to evaluate soundly everything they subsequently learn about themselves, their fellowmen and the complex world men have made. They will need much experience in making such judgments and evaluations before they will make with assurance truly Christian decisions that accord with their God-created humanity. But they will have been given a solid foundation upon which to build their lives.

Although I firmly believe that Catholic high school education is far more important than Catholic grade school education, the whole thrust of this book is that we should never have to choose to support the one and not the other.

Before ending the discussion of the high schools and beginning the discussion of the higher institutions of learning, I would like to refer to the debate about the merits and place of physical training, and particularly of organized sports, in the schools. There is little opposition to physical training on a voluntary and medically monitored basis. Organized sports are good—good for the participants and good for the schools. Perhaps the sports should be open to more participants—extended to adequately coached teams of less competence than the regular squad—and certainly fewer aspects of professionalism should be permitted. But good athletic teams lend an important element of prestige to a school and contribute to the student's pride and joy in attending that school. Man does not live by bread or books alone. He needs not only prayer but play for complete health of body and soul. Spectators as well as participants are at play at a game and quite obviously derive exhilaration and relaxation out of it. De-emphasis of sports is neither natural nor Christian.

Catholic Universities and Colleges

Some predict that within 35 years there will be twice as many young people in our country as there are today, and that more than half of those of college age will attend colleges or universities. Attendance is already approaching the half-way mark. Whether or not Catholic colleges and universities will maintain their present enrollment percentage (one-sixth) of Catholic college students is impossible to predict. It is certain, however, that the absolute number of students in Catholic colleges and universities will be much greater, possibly double. The importance of this field of Catholic education, therefore, cannot be overemphasized. It will be a growth industry if it maintains its relative attractiveness.

Most college students, physiologically, are adults. Mentally, emotionally and morally, however, important finishing touches are needed. The great debate has always been about the role of the institutions of higher learning in supplying those finishing touches. In our day the secular institutions seem to have agreed that their role is solely the intellectual development of young people. They take them and leave them as they find them emotionally and morally, although they enforce a kind of morality through disciplinary rules designed to maintain sufficient order to permit academic learning to be quietly and uninterruptedly pursued. The in loco parentis role has been abandoned.

Within this general area of agreement the secular institutions vary considerably in what they consider necessary to the maintenance of adequate peace and order. Some students accuse their college of approaching too closely the role of parents who view their children as adolescents. Some parents say that college administrators give too much freedom to the students to make decisions the parents believe late-adolescents should not be trusted to make. It is obvious, however, that the problem is considered a practical one of discipline only, and not as one involving any obligation of the institutions to teach morality as such, much less religious values.

Catholic universities and colleges take a different view of their role. On the premise that a student is a body-soul, they take a pastoral as well as an academic view of the matter and continue the preparation of students to take their places in the world as whole, authentic humans. This view has been severely criticized. Those who hold that intellectual formation and the imparting of knowledge are the only proper functions of an institution of higher learning summarize their position briefly and bluntly: "A Catholic university is a contradiction in terms." In this view, a university or college must be open to all truth and all views of truth and plump for none. Catholicism, on the other hand, is only one view of truth. Accordingly, an institution which teaches truth from the viewpoint of Catholicism is not open and cannot claim to be a university or college in an acceptable sense.

Before Vatican II these critics could cite many examples to justify the charge that only the Catholic line was propagated on Catholic campuses. Unfortunately, there have been a few similar examples to point to since Vatican II. Some Church authorities still seem to view Catholic universities and colleges as primarily pastoral (with strong connotations of protective and defensive) arms of the Church. They seem to be unable to understand or agree with the concept of academic freedom which most of the Catholic institutions themselves have come to share with their secular counterparts. It seems likely that the Church authorities and the institutions will through earnest and sincere dialog reach a common understanding on the issue in the not too distant future. It is the institutions themselves, of course, which will have to think the matter through first. They are aware of this, and several groups of them—on even an international scale—have developed tentative statements of a position which is intelligible and explainable as Catholic, and thus different from secular, and yet open, and thus academically free. One such statement is now under discussion at the Vatican itself.

To make their position more credible, some seem to think it advisable to move to a legal status of independence from all official Church structures, or even religious orders, to a position of freedom from make-or-break financial dependence upon any such structure or religious order. Yet this seems an exaggerated solution to the problem of academic freedom. The college officials and the authorities of the diocese or religious order which owns it should agree to principles of operation which would make such a legal separation unnecessary. The legal separation of universities and colleges from sponsoring religious entities is presently taking place more out of considerations of potential governmental aid than out of concern for academic freedom. This step will not accomplish its purpose if the institution, though no longer legally Catholic, or Jesuit, remains in purpose and practice committed to Catholic intellectual, moral, or integrated religious-secular formation or atmosphere.

A satisfactory position with respect to academic freedom for a Catholic university or college would be comparable to the new view of truth taken by Vatican II, that is, the view that the Church has few absolute, eternal answers. The Church may not even know the right questions at any given moment in history. But it believes it has some answers, and it is constantly searching for more or better ones.

The Catholic universities and colleges, therefore, could say with the Church: "We search for the right questions and the right answers. We are not always sure we have either. Today, this and this is the way they look to us. From this vantage point, we draw such and such implications for this field of learning and for that. We will continue to explore with the rest of mankind other questions, other answers and other implications. We will test all against only one standard—the Scriptures and our traditions—but we will put even the Scriptures and traditions to the test of all other sources of truth. We are dedicated to the search for truth about man, answers to his eternal questions about himself and the world in which he finds himself and solutions to his problems of living in an increasingly complex society. But, yes, we do start from a position. We believe we know enough about these matters to provide a sound basis for guiding men in practical affairs. As long as we remain dedicated to open search for a better basis, or the same basis better understood, we believe we are fulfilling a role of greater benefit to men than if we adopted a position of total ignorance about man's origin and destiny, knowing nothing and unable to learn anything for the practical guidance of men, here and now, in fulfilling their nature."

With such a position and purpose, Catholic universities and colleges would, for one thing, be nonagnostic, nonskeptical, noncynical think factories. The universities should have strong schools of theology designed to assist the Church to ask the right questions and work out the right answers, and to furnish the other schools of the university with insights in their search for truth. They should also have schools of education to help grade and high schools and the CCD projects for children and adults to improve and keep up-to-date the content and methods of teaching. Economics, sociology and political science departments should watch-dog all economic, social and political institutions, not only critically but creatively. They should develop practical suggestions for improving institutions and living conditions, especially in urban areas, so that they respect the nature and dignity of all men. Physical and biological science departments should explore man and his environment to improve both in the light of insights suggested by traditional Christian beliefs.

It would not be unreasonable, for instance, for scientists in a Catholic university to theorize with the assistance of theologians and then to devise research projects to determine, how the world might end, or how it might pass naturally from its present state into another which would support a different kind of life, including resurrected human beings. Scientists and theologians could discuss how men's bodies will be raised from the dead and be eternally reunited to their souls (by some affective power of their souls?) in a new, natural world amounting to heaven; how and where Christ may be living today in His glorified body; the nature of Teilhard de Chardin's "inward principle of matter" that may have brought about evolution from simplicity to greater and greater complexity and may end in a perfection of all things that could be eternal; whether "evil" is a correct concept, or whether and how it may be functional and thus in a sense "good" from a long-range, broad, God's-eye point of view. Breakthroughs in scientific and theological knowledge have resulted from theories and questions no stranger than these.

The universities and the colleges might well assign trained theologians to each major academic division to achieve easy day-to-day communication and mutual assistance in keeping the integration of the religious and the secular in all disciplines up-to-date.

Hopefully, the thought products of the universities will be assisted by and used by all for whose benefit they are developed, such as the hierarchy, the lower schools, and the business, political and professional communities. Communication between the academic and the outside communities should be improved. Academia, not just the Church, suffers from ivory tower tendencies.

But Catholic universities and colleges should be more than think factories developing information only for export. No one has accused them of believing that their first responsibility is to research rather than to students. It is unlikely that Catholic institutions will ever fall into that educational heresy. Their teaching staffs will remain primarily teachers, not primarily researchers and book writers. The charge that they are too pastoral should indicate that no one will charge them with indifference to their students' total needs, or that the curriculum is incompetent, immaterial, and irrelevant, an impersonal injection of facts which may well be obsolete before the students can use them in the world of business and politics. Catholic universities and colleges will teach their students how to observe, judge and act as free intelligent men. They will not condition them to be slaves of machines or victims of institutions.

Of course, this is more easily said than done. How will the open pursuit of truth move from the Catholic university level to the student in the classroom? Schools of education must continually work on this problem. Hopefully, the men who staff these schools will show a positive attitude by trying to find ways to introduce Christian values without violating academic freedom instead of trying to show that Catholic philosophy should be rigorously excluded from the classroom. Educational experts should be accepted with honor on their own campuses, and should be admitted to dialog with their colleagues in the other departments and in other educational institutions. Out of such cooperative effort might come a permanent system of interdisciplinary cross-fertilization of knowledge and ideas and the transmission of them to the students by team teaching.

Classroom technique should certainly emphasize presentation rather than indoctrination. Christian truth will be presented by men who know it, believe it and live it. Other views of truth will be similarly presented. An important technique will be dialog with the students themselves in classrooms and outside them to ensure that students understand the subject matter, and also to get their views concerning curricula based on values other than purely economic ones. High academic standards will not be compromised, but innovative means of assisting students to meet them will become a particular mark of Catholic institutions of higher learning. There will be pastoral activities to motivate students to commitment or recommitment, but they will be conducted outside the classroom. Even in pastoral activities the emphasis will be on preaching and teaching the Gospel and on helping the students to grow up intellectually and emotionally so as to free them, humanly speaking, from obstacles to accepting faith as a gift of God. A number of Catholic universities and colleges are experimenting with "campus ministries," with professional personnel and imaginative pastoral programs.

Some universities and colleges, both religious and secular, have started to experiment with councils composed of appointed or elected representatives of the faculty, the students and the administrators. Their purpose is to achieve consensus on policy matters of common concern. Some reach into such sticky matters as the general direction of the curriculum, the selection and tenure of faculty and staff and student disciplinary rules and penalties. Catholic institutions should have much to contribute to this development. They should have a better idea of community than their secular counterparts and better tools (the Christian virtues) for achieving it. Presumably, the experimenters are aware of the legal limits of a council's authority compared to the authority of the board of directors or trustees of the institution. Without this clear understanding, there could be trouble. Should alumni be represented on such a council as part of the academic community? Or should they be left to their nostalgic memories, their football ticket preferences based on their financial contributions and take to their graves their prejudices about campus activists?

CCD Programs for Children

Programs for the religious formation of public school grade and high school children are more difficult to design than those for children in the Catholic schools because two factors are inherent in the situation. Since these factors will always be present, special efforts must always be exerted to overcome them.

The first difficulty is that religious education cannot be directly integrated with secular education because the children study secular subjects at a different time and place. Religious education must be "poured over" the secular education, so to speak. This is a most difficult task because the secular education seems to the children to be complete and sufficient of itself. The children resist any suggestion by CCD teachers that the learning supplied by the children's public school teachers is incomplete.

The second difficulty with CCD education is that it is at very least an unpopular imposition on the children's time. At worst it is an unpopular social and cultural activity which sets the children off from most of their peer group. It's strange that those who deplore the Catholic schools as "divisive" and "ghetto-ish" do not seem to have the same attitude about CCD classes. Imposed, resented attendance is not favorable to learning. This factor is particularly significant among high school adolescents where peer group pressures toward conformity are strong.

These two difficulties must, nevertheless, be overcome to the greatest possible extent. The situation demands stronger programming. Interest must be engendered without allowing the program to degenerate into mere entertainment. Basic catechism must be taught just as it is in the schools. Teachers should not use the old Baltimore Catechism method of teaching by rote. Instead, they should use the kerygmatic method, relying heavily upon Bible study and the application of religious truths and values to everyday life situations. They should treat all aspects and problems of life in keeping with the children's age and experience.

The children should discuss their secular subjects, and teachers should correlate the secular with religious values, observations and insights. Directors of CCD classes are not making much progress in this area at the present time. Although the programs do cover everything else the children learn from their friends, the radio and TV, the movies, etc., they are not correlated with the subjects taught in public schools. Some time should be spent in CCD classes reviewing the actual class work of the students in the previous week, adding Christian value judgments and pointing out the relevance of Christian truths to what the students have been taught. Directors of each local CCD program should analyze the standard textbooks used in the public schools in their community and provide the CCD teachers with appropriate study guides for class review and discussion of the material appearing in the textbooks. The teachers—preferably a team of teachers with appropriate academic backgrounds—would then handle the subjects as the students currently report on them.

Many of the larger publishers of standard textbooks design an edition of the same book adapted for use in Catholic schools. These firms might design a "relevance" series of pamphlets, corresponding to each standard textbook, which could be used as teaching aids in CCD courses. Such pamphlets would be inexpensive and could do a good job of annotating the textbooks by presenting Catholic positions or "what do you think of that" questions, on a page by page or subject by subject basis.

One of the most essential elements of CCD programming is personnel. It is particularly important that the people who design the courses, supervise the establishment and assist in the maintenance of particular projects be competent educators and administrators. They should be dedicated to the work, and they should be paid competitive salaries. To date, CCD teachers have been recruited on a voluntary basis. Most of them have been lay men and women willing to devote a year or two or three to teaching children's groups once a week. Some programs have suffered as much from the absence of teachers on scheduled class days as from absence of students. Effective programming is impossible on such a haphazard basis. A diocese determined to have an effective CCD program will probably find it necessary to engage permanent, well-trained teachers who are paid adequate salaries.

In this section we are discussing only programs. It is impossible today to say whether or not CCD programs for children are failing— as they admittedly are—because of faulty programming or because of general apathy on the part of the Catholic community which is reflected in the lack of resources for the programs. In the long run, programming must be good or resources will dry up. But good programs cannot be developed to begin with, or be carried on long enough to correct the errors without adequate resources of personnel and money.

This vicious circle must be broken by a concerted effort of the Catholic community to marshal the necessary resources. It seems unlikely that this will be done unless and until parish and diocesan councils are established. Only such structures will involve *all* parents. Members can budget resources for the schools and the CCD programs, or resolve the priorities if resources prove to be insufficient for both.

These matters are treated more fully in the next two chapters of this book. In the long run it would be found more economical to pursue the old goal of every Catholic child in a Catholic school than to support schools for half of the children and CCD programs for the other half. Even if such a goal should prove to be realistic, however, it could not be achieved for 30 or 40 years. In the meantime, we must have a strong, adequately supported CCD program, and we must see to it that all Catholic children who are in public grade and high schools attend CCD classes.

Programs for Secular Campuses

The aim of chaplaincies and Newman apostolates on secular campuses is to help Catholic students there to keep their faith, deepen it and make it meaningful in their adult lives. About five-sixths of Catholic students attending universities and colleges are on secular campuses, mostly state-supported ones.

The problem of integrating religion with secular subjects is the same as that which exists in public grade and high schools—it must be done separately from the secular teaching. Formal catechism courses are seldom given. For one thing, sufficient personnel to give such courses is lacking. So chaplains must assume that the students have had religious instruction in their grade and high school years, that they have acquired basic religious information and have formed good religious attitudes. But Catholic chaplains on secular campuses have found that this assumption is false. The number of Catholic students who are committed Christians or even well-instructed Christians is appallingly small. Religion instructors and advisors on Catholic campuses have found the same thing to be true.

In any event, because of shortage of manpower and difficulties inherent in the situation, Newman apostolate programs are limited to sermons, lectures, personal counseling and group discussions geared to the adult intellectual and emotional level of the students. Action programs directed to meaningful involvement in religious and civic affairs are developed. The organization and success of such activities depends upon the numbers and qualifications of the priests, religious or laymen assigned to the apostolate by the bishop. These people are supposed to be qualified to meet the students where they are intellectually, emotionally and culturally. Physical resources are a minor requirement of this work. Even chapels and meeting rooms can be obtained on a shared basis.

The very terms used for Catholic educational ventures on secular campuses: "mission," and "apostolate"—indicate two deplorable facts: the field is large but the laborers are few; and the work is difficult and similar to that required in pagan mission territories. Failure to make a concerted effort to provide men and money for this huge field of Catholic education is a reproach to the faith and charity of the Catholic community.

Within 35 years the number of young people attending colleges and universities will be two or three times the number attending today. Yet, if present trends continue, the percentage of Catholic students enrolled in Catholic colleges and universities will decline. If both of these estimates prove to be substantially accurate, the size of the problem of adequately reaching Catholic students on secular campuses will be tremendously increased.

Programs for Adults

There are two compelling reasons why adults need religious education: first, to provide them with adult-level knowledge about Catholic truths so as to strengthen their personal commitment to Christian living in a world which increasingly confronts them with challenges to their faith and confusing situations for application of Christian principles; and second, to enable them to instruct their children in Christian truths and guide them in application of Christian values to the real life situations the children are encountering.

The Church must be an adult Church, not a Church only for adults, of course, but a Church in which adults have a mature attitude toward religion which they can in turn pass on to their children. Those who say that we can get along very well without Catholic schools stress this latter goal vigorously. They argue that the Catholic education of children is the responsibility of parents, that the home is the specific instrument designed by God Himself for providing such personal and essential formation of children and that the natural ability to accomplish this is somehow infused by the Holy Spirit along with the spiritual graces of the Sacrament of Matrimony.

In the previous section we gave the only empirical evidence of the value of the home versus the school in achieving the Christian formation of children when we reported surveys which show that Catholic school education seems to take better among children from homes which are themselves religious. Presumably, this means homes where the parents support what the children are being taught in the schools by indicating their agreement with it and by making a sincere effort to live their Christian faith and thus provide a Christian environment and example to the children.

Such a finding is hardly astonishing. When good literature, or true art or higher values in anything else taught in school are not appreciated in a particular home and may even be derided there, the children do not learn to appreciate the subject as well as children from homes having a more supportive attitude. Yet they learn about the subject and may learn to appreciate it by themselves later. A generation of children 50 years ago learned a great deal despite the attitude of most of their parents that most learning was useless because the boys were going to work at sixteen, and the girls were going to get married sooner or later. In any event, the finding is hardly evidence that parents could perform by themselves the entire job of religious education.

One trouble with educational programs for adults is that they are voluntary, and great difficulty is encountered in getting adults to attend lecture or study programs. There are at least two reasons why this is so. For one thing, parents have a legitimate reason for not attending more than one or two, or a short series of lectures now and then. They are really too busy with family affairs and business and social obligations. For another thing, most of today's real life adults (and presumably these are the ones we are concerned about, not tomorrow's adults, or adults as ivory tower idealists imagine or wish them to be) see no reason for attending religious education programs. If we were buttonholed by a zealous soul trying to organize a lecture series, most of us would say we know enough about that stuff; we're doing all right just as we are, etc. For many, if not most adults, the Vatican II type of religious education is unsettling, even annoying. They purposely evade exposure to it. Adult religious education programs are attended by persons who least need them, and by no others.

Yet we must certainly have an adult Church whose members understand what it is to be mature, authentic Christians and are, therefore, qualified to help children to become mature, authentic, Christian adults. What, then, can be done besides encouraging good sermons and a strong Catholic press?

There are two types of educational programs. One is the presentation of informational material. In the field of adult education this suggests lectures and study programs. The other type is on-the-job training, learning by doing. This suggests action programs for adults designed to teach Christian values and principles by engaging adults in real-life situations that require the application of such values and principles.

At least 99.44% of our difficulties these days stem from the fact that adults are not adult in even the natural order. We do not know ourselves very well. We do not understand our neighbors. We would like to believe we understand our children, but we gradually realize that we do not.

Our religious instructors taught us that anyone can be good if he just wills to be good. We know little or nothing about the influences of heredity, the way we were brought up and the forgotten experiences of our lives which make it impossible for us calmly and successfully to pursue the purpose of being good. We do not understand why the war of the spirit against the flesh so often and unaccountably ends in the victory of the flesh. We do not realize that many of us distrust or actually dislike ourselves, and that if we hold ourselves in low esteem, little that is constructive can come out of our relations with our children and our neighbors. We are constantly depressed by doing, not what we would, but what we would not. We do not know how to communicate well even with our spouses, much less with our children or our neighbors. We despair of making a community out of our own households, and so we feel hypocritical when we talk about making a community out of our parish, our city, our nation or the world. We say: "If only I were a better Christian; if only my children would obey the commandments; if only all citizens would obey the Golden Rule, then everything would be all right." We do not realize the underlying natural human factors that make this view too simplistic. We need to know more about ourselves in order to make our wills effectively free.

Catholic educational programs for adults would produce the best results and be best attended if they were devoted exclusively to the things our novelists, poets and other prophets have been telling us about ourselves and our society, and which the psychiatrists, the psychologists and the sociologists confirm. These matters would be presented so as to show the relationship of Christian truths to them, and vice versa, so that the full picture of authentic man would emerge. What becomes a Christian is a man. No man becomes an authentic Christian unless he first becomes a mature man. "Grace builds on nature." We men are the most important, and not the least mysterious, element of the world given to us to understand and subdue.

So far as courses and study group programs are concerned, that would be it. Valuable? Fundamental, Popular? People hunger for it.

A program of Christian education by involvement will exist when parish and diosesan councils are established as recommended by

Vatican II and described in the following chapter of this book. To make our present point it is only necessary to look at some of the matters that would be handled by the councils: liturgy, family life, parish social activities, education of children and adults, ecumenical activities, social action, civic community affairs. These matters would be assigned to committees whose membership would extend beyond the council members themselves. Each committee would have as many members of the parish or diocesan community as were interested in the committee's subject and either had some competence in the subject or were willing to learn about it. Constant but not too frequent turnover of council and committee membership would be arranged. Every proposed decision would be discussed in terms of the relevant facts and the pertinent Christian principles. In the first place, therefore, there would be discussion, and hence education, on what were the pertinent Christian principles. And in the end practical Christian means would have to be devised for giving effect to the principles in the Christian action agreed upon.

This description of the operation of councils is a description of a learn-by-doing educational program. No more effective method of educating exists. The councils would provide two-directional education, one toward each individual involved in the processes of decision-making and action, one toward the group. Each person would learn interpersonal Christian virtues, and all of them would learn how to become a Christian community. This is the fullness of Christian education for adults of our time.

The Disadvantaged

The prime objective of Catholic education is not only to teach Catholic truths but to teach the application of those truths to every aspect and problem of life. Life as it exists and the problems encountered by children and adults in the inner city differ not only in degree but in kind from those encountered by others. Religious education programs for them must take these differences into account, or they will be irrelevant. Secular education is subject to the same requirement. Energy and resources will be wasted and social results will be disastrous if educators forget this.

This field of education more than any other requires intelligent experimentation in content and method. Communicated love and respect for the dignity of people, as well as understanding and compassion is certain to pay the greatest dividends.

The most important recommendation about programs for children and adults in this special field is that there be a qualified central agency preferably within the diocesan office of education whose task is to establish, support and guide such programs. Central personnel would coordinate the efforts of all groups engaged in the programs, help plan the programs, help procure qualified personnel and appropriate facilities and keep in touch with results so that changing needs can be quickly recognized and promptly met with balance and effectiveness.

The emphasis in the role of the central agency should be on the spirit expressed in the terms, "advise and assist," "counsel and help." If the central agency is manned as it should be with qualified professional educators, it should be open to experimentation and dialog with the people personally affected. Openness to experimentation, new departures and radical changes are essential in this challenging field of education. Programs must be pursued competently, confidently and prudently but with openness. We must start from the position that we have some of the answers but not all of them. We must persevere in the firm attitude that we do not own the poor. We are not entitled to have them always with us in order to have a constant supply of objects upon which to bestow charity so that we may grow in virtue. The poor own us and are entitled to the kind of help from us that will enable them to help themselves to be no longer poor and dependent upon charity.

This is the one field of all fields of education in which the Catholic community can lead the civic community. Unfortunately and disgracefully, Catholic educators have left to others too many opportunities to lead and serve the poor. Too often the first schools to be abandoned by the Catholic community have been those in the inner city. If we were true Christians dedicated to following our Master's injunction to preach the good news to the poor, the inner city schools are the last ones we would close. (This is a purely rhetorical statement. We should not have to make that either-or choice.) If we accepted our responsibility to lead the world to sanity, peace and brotherhood under the fatherhood of God, we would lead with ideas and programs to meet the educational problems of the inner city.

The root of these problems is the deep conviction on the part of the people involved that education is valueless and learning is useless. Surely the Catholic Church knows why men should bother to learn and has ideas concerning what are the most important things to learn. The most significant thing most people in the inner city need to learn is precisely why they should learn any part of what the academic world calls secular knowledge. The significance of such learning as a religious obligation shown by integrated religious-secular education is a specific way to help these people. Only in a religious school can children and adolescents learn that they are persons of unique value and dignity, and that they should learn for the love of God and the accomplishment of his will on earth as well as in heaven. In no other school is there a chance to convince them through the very manner and spirit of the teaching that they should learn to make the best possible use of the talents the good Lord has given them, and that sooner or later they will find a way to use those talents for their own happiness and welfare and for the happiness and welfare of their loved ones and their neighbors.

So far as the physically handicapped are concerned, the problems are chiefly limited to the difficulty of getting the children to the school. The school needs to provide only a welcoming atmosphere. However, if the defect is one of sight, hearing or speech, special provisions should be made to detect and cope with the impairment rather than to turn the child over to the public school system. Experts in these fields can be employed by the Catholic school system to ride the circuit of the schools, just as they are in the public school system.

The mentally handicapped present a problem in the field of the corporal works of mercy rather than in the field of education. Hence, it is outside the scope of this book. Hospital and nursing care are not generally considered to be activities within the Church's mission to preach and teach. Catholic institutions which care for mentally retarded children are not usually considered part of the Church's educational structure even though they do their best to form the children as Christian citizens so far as the understanding of the children will permit.

Finally, there is the question of what the Catholic community should do about the education of the delinquent child. It assuredly is a subject within the scope of this book. Quoting Tevye of *Fiddler on the Roof* fame: "On the one hand . . . but on the other hand . . . ." On the one hand is the argument of charity toward the delinquent child. On the other hand is the rotten-apple-in-the-barrel argument. "I'll tell you the answer. I don't know." Expert opinion, dialog and trial and error will probably develop the best Christian approach. In the meantime, we hope that Catholic educators will walk a long road with any child before writing him off as truly delinquent.

One basic theme runs through this book. Beginning with Father Greeley's chapters on a theology of Catholic education through the chapters on purpose and programs, we have stressed the point that learning for human beings should embrace all that needs to be known and done by people and society to make of each individual and of society fully what their Creator intended them to be. True learning, complete learning, therefore, is a composite of all of the academic disciplines and practical arts—science, the humanities, engineering, medicine, jurisprudence, politics, economics and religion. Learning is a seamless garment of many colors.

No individual is able to master all knowledge. The wise man is he who knows that he should learn what he can about everything as well as everything he can about one thing. He learns first and foremost to relate to each other the bits of knowledge, great or small, which he is able to master. He is fortunate if he lives in a time when society values this kind of wisdom. In such a society the scientist, the humanist, the physician, the lawyer and the theologian work together because they know that each has a contribution to make to the other and to the total wisdom about man. Together they advance the learning of men and develop the seamless, vari-colored garment of collective wisdom. Wisdom should be learned that way, and it should be taught that way.

5. The Renovation of Structures

Without love a man is but a sounding brass and a clashing cymbal. Without structure a human venture is but a babble of tongues and a disorganized exercise in futility. In an individual man, love directs power. In a society of men, structure integrates and synergizes power. In a Christian community, structure mobilizes, concentrates and directs like a laser beam the power of its members' love.

The great Jewish scholar Maimonides wrote in the twelfth century that charity has seven levels. The lowest is face-to-face almsgiving. The highest is assisting to develop a system that provides poor men with the means of so helping themselves that they no longer need alms. The latter concept of charity has been given Christian recognition most recently in the social encyclicals of the modern popes who have been pleading for systems, institutions and organizations to help men and nations of men to help themselves.

An Adaptable Structure Is Necessary

Structure is essential. It is the organizing and integrating principle of any human venture. The term suffers a bad connotation of rigidity, inflexibility and impersonality. To the extent that structures are rigid, inflexible and impersonal they are also dysfunctional, but they do not have to be either rigid, inflexible or impersonal.

Structure is the system that any group of people, even as small and close-knit as a family, uses to come to decisions about what to do and how to do it, and to assign the tasks—from supervisory to

110

menial—to get it done. Of course, the system can be poorly formed at the beginning, or it can become ineffective in the course of its operation. When it turns out to be inefficient, it should and can be renovated or even replaced. But some structure will be required if the venture is to continue.

The Catholic educational mission is a human venture involving the people of God. What system, what structure should the people of God establish to make and to implement decisions about how to educate each other and their children as People of God? We do not want structure for structure's sake or organization for organization's sake. That is a game we too often play because we have a passion for ordering everything. We want structure with a sense of purpose.

How shall we examine and continually reexamine the purpose of Catholic education? How shall we implement that purpose through specific programs to reach all people where they are? How shall we gather resources of men and materials and deploy them to operate the programs and ascertain whether the programs are accomplishing our purpose? If they are not, what means shall we adopt to change the programs and realign the resources? These decisions must be made by people acting together to accomplish a purpose which is important and complex and needs constant adjustments to succeed.

Underlying and supporting everything described in this book, therefore, must be structure. It must not be rigid, inflexible or impersonal. It must be open and adaptable to meet the changing conditions that will confront the educational venture down the years. Its openness and flexibility should be built-in features to assure constant response to the changing educational needs of the people it is designed to serve and to the changing conditions which may affect the manner in which those human needs can best be met.

We have a structure for these purposes, but not the kind advocated in this book which criticizes the present structure as a non-system, a nonstructure. We will advocate moving to a system, minimal but adequate.

The Structure for Education Must Fit Church Structure

The Church's educational venture, the formation of authentic Christians through teaching the Word of God and its implications, is only one of the Church's activities. It is such a vital activity, however, so central to the nature and purpose of the Church, that it must not be treated in isolation as if it were an autonomous operation. Structurally, it could be handled as an autonomous operation for a while. And in many places it may have to be so handled in order to do the good that can be done *now* instead of waiting to do the better. But ultimately, a philosophy of structure should be identical in both the Church overall and in its educational venture. Furthermore, both the Church as a whole and its educational venture should develop actual structures which fit each other, the educational structure fitting *within* the overall structure.

For this reason it seems well to present some preliminary thoughts concerning structure for the Church as a whole, and then consider structure for education and show how the latter might fit into the former.

Present Church Structures Are Inappropriate

Only a few years ago we read that business management experts highly praised the Church's structure. They explained that they were interested in the Roman Catholic Church because an organization that had been "in business" nearly 2,000 years must be "well managed." It was easy for them to find an "ideal chain of command" from parish priest through bishop to pope and "efficient handling of administrative details" by its "superb bureaucracy."

Today there is widespread criticism of the Church's structure. If the criticism is justified, the experts were wrong in the first place; the Church is no longer "well managed," or both of the first two possibilities are true. The criticism is justified for both reasons.

When the Second Vatican Council restated the nature and purpose of the Church in concepts that had not been adverted to in centuries, both the praise and the validity of the old structure became passé. The management experts, therefore, were not wrong in their appraisal of the Church's structure in the light of the nature and purpose of the Church as described to them at the time. The nature and the purpose of an institution is where management experts always start when appraising the structure of the institution.

Because structure is functional, the only question is whether the one designed for a particular venture accomplishes its purpose with a maximum of justice to its participants and a minimum of confusion among them. A business venture stresses efficiency. A political or social venture tolerates a good deal of inefficiency. This is especially true when the development of responsible human freedom is its chief purpose—as it is in the Church.

In the light of Vatican II decisions are being made in the wrong way, in view of the nature and purpose of the Church. The Church is a democratic community, or more accurately, as we shall see presently, it was made constitutionally democratic by its founder. For a democratic Church, simple hierarchical order is good structure, but it is not adequate because decisions are too narrowly based, and their implementation does not sufficiently allow for the free working of the Holy Spirit among the Church's members. Bureaucracy is good structure except when it makes the decisions instead of administering them.

Vatican II reminded us that the Church is by nature a democratic as well as a hierarchical institution because it is made up of human beings of equal dignity among whom the Spirit breathes where he wills. The lowliest layman may be given a truth, or an insight leading to a truth which he is obliged to share with his fellows and which they are obliged to consider so that there may be unity in advancement toward him who is all truth. Yet there is no provision for such communication in the present structure of the Church.

The Second Vatican Council's reference to agencies set up by the Church to enable the laity to express opinions for the good of the Church has a very hollow sound. A bishop who asks the laity to supply funds for a television station to enable him to communicate to them is not supplying the two-way communication specified by Vatican II. Television is modern, but such use of it may perpetuate an ancient defect in structure. The modern streamlining of the United States Catholic Conference by the bishops could prove to be similarly negative. In a democratic society, two-way channels of communication are as essential a part of the structure as are channels of authority. The structure should be designed so that the functions of communication and authority are accomplished by all concerned in one motion.

But to advocate abolishing an existing structure because of its faults is not enlightened or courageous. It is fruitless. To advocate abolishing all structure is not radical; it is anarchical. To advocate returning to the simple structure of the early Church is not progressive; it is retrogressive, and nothing could be better calculated to bring impotence and diaspora upon the Church. A loosely structured, dispersed Church would be an invisible, inaudible witness. Ineffectiveness in and toward the world is not supposed to be a mark of Christ's Church. Restructure, yes; destructure, no!

Prudence is that virtue which is directed to action, not to study and counsel, although a reasonable amount of the latter is an integral part of it. Prudence deals with ways and means and down-to-earth realities. It is accurately and completely expressed in the Cardijn formula quoted with approval by Pope John XXIII: "Observe, judge, act." It is a virtue to be practiced not only by individuals but also by groups, organizations, bodies politic and by the Church. Obviously, its mode of practice by groups differs from that by individuals. Its practice by groups requires structure.

Christ left his followers no blueprint for structure. He left only the clear implication that the Christian community should have designated leaders. The early Church had a negligible structure. It was a small community whose members met, considered and acted together. As the Church grew, bishops and popes made prudential decisions that affected more than one local community just as leaders of the political bodies of the time, especially the Roman empire made decisions. The Church is and always has been a corporal as well as a spiritual body whose members are people of their time. For centuries monarchy was all they understood. And monarchy cannot be surpassed for simplicity of structure. But in our time we have come to realize that democratic societies, once they can no

THE RENOVATION OF STRUCTURES

longer fit into a town hall, require more elaborate structure than monarchy.

The Holy Spirit sees to it that defined doctrine is kept pure, but he does not dictate when and by what means doctrine is to be defined. The Eucharist and the other sacraments are his, but he leaves it to men to determine to whom, when, and in what form they are to be administered. Christian truth is his, but he leaves it to men to explore all of its implications and to decide how to act in accordance with it. He helps all men to commit themselves to his truths and to cooperate with his graces, but he leaves it to men to carry his message and in vast part his graces to other men.

Hence, the problem of structure must not be left to the Holy Spirit. To do so would be presumptuous. Apropos this point is the famous statement (slightly expanded) of Edmund Burke: "All that is necessary for evil or stupidity to prevail is for all men of good will and common sense to do nothing"—except pray!

What happens when a modern corporation is confronted with a technological development or shift in market preference which threatens the corporation's existence? If the directors are incompetent or frightened men, they find themselves presiding over the bankruptcy of the corporation. If they are competent and courageous, they guide a reorganization of the corporation.

The first thing they do is reexamine and update the purpose of the corporation. Next they determine what physical changes must take place and how to go about it. Then they move into the new action. Changes are not made for their own sake, but neither are changes indicated by the new conditions deferred because "we have always done it this way."

When the buggy makers of old converted to automobiles, the directors and chief executive officers made all of the decisions and told their people in detail what their new jobs were. The technique of management has advanced considerably since then. Insights like sensitivity and motivation have been gained. Executives are aware of the practical advisability of being sensitive to the dignity and freedom of men and to the subtle as well as the obvious things that motivate or discourage particular men. Today a large corporation is not turned around simply by fiat from on high. Neither does it conduct its day-to-day operations or handle its brush-fire problems by the old bull-of-the-woods method. Modern management uses the techniques of participative management and management by objective.

Important final decisions and authority to enforce them are still in the hands of top management. But the decisions are made in consultation with the next level or two of management. The latter explain purpose, define roles (jobs) and gain the understanding and acceptance of the men below them, and so on down the line. In this way not only are better decisions made, but the people who are to carry them out understand what they are expected to accomplish. They are given appropriately broad discretion on how to do so and go about their tasks with enthusiasm. The keys to this technique are the defining and redefining of the overall purpose of the organization, and the defining and redefining of the roles to be played by each individual to achieve it—all by appropriate participation of those engaged in the venture.

The skeleton structure of business organizations has not changed. There is still a top boss, levels of management below him, and the rank and file. But even top management is recognized to be a type of service. More importantly, the skeleton structure has been supplied with a completely new nervous system called channels of communication. Business calls the result of good communication integration or coordination of the organization. The venture is planned, organized and coordinated by all concerned through a known, visible, structured communication system. The communication system is not allowed to break down. It is continually checked to make certain that it is open and effectively used in all directions. By this means, awareness of change within and outside the organization is quick and constant, permitting continual adjustment of operations. Modern corporations are seldom caught with obsolete products or irrelevant responses to public opinion.

If these concepts and techniques based upon the nature of man work like fire in the wet wood of secular enterprises, how much better should they work in the dry wood of religious ones!

The Church is not a business organization in the ordinary sense. But it has a business, that is, a purpose. And it is an organization of men using human and temporal resources to achieve its purpose. It is like a business firm whose officers and employees are also the members or stockholders, and whose purpose is to make products and provide services for the officers, members and general community. It is more akin to the cooperative form of business than to the corporation form.

The Concept of Conciliar Structure

According to Vatican II, the Church's purpose is to bring all men to a common destiny of eternal happiness by recreating the world by Christianizing it, that is, to make the Church's own members whole and holy chiefly by making other men and human society whole and holy. Vatican II recognized the importance of defining roles to achieve this purpose and suggested major guidelines for each essential role with special emphasis on the role of the laity.

Vatican II's most significant recommendation relating directly to the structure of the Church, and the agencies for communication within it, was that councils be established at all levels: parochial (parish), interparochial (deanery, vicariate, etc.), diocesan, interdiocesan (provincial), national, and international (continental, Vatican).

If such Councils are broadly established, there will exist a structure for resolving the major problems in the Church today and tomorrow. At each appropriate level all the people of God—hierarchy, priests, religious and laity—will be represented at the same table. They will not only discuss problems but they will agree upon programs of action and assign responsibilities for carrying them out. This will constitute adult education of the most effective kind, for everyone involved will learn Christian principles, help devise Christian applications to particular problems, and through the very process of discussion and confrontation develop Christian virtues of love and respect for himself and his neighbors.

It is difficult to imagine a better means for developing an effective understanding of the nature and purpose of the Church and the proper roles of its several members, for broadening the concept of the Church's mission now in this particular place and for developing

Christian action programs and engaging everyone in specific tasks to carry them out. Monarchical structure may have been appropriate in its day because none other would have been understood. But today, even in the very parts of the world where Christianity is strongest, monarchy is resented and resisted. Trust in the intelligence and responsible freedom of man rooted in the dignity of his person is the basic thrust of Christianity.

It is inconceivable that the will of God will be done in these times either by fiat from the hierarchy or by the clash of group pressures. It is tragic that good Christians should feel obliged to "do their thing" outside the institutional Church instead of within it. Priests, religious and laity should not have to experiment surreptitiously with what they believe are more relevant and meaningful liturgical forms. They should not have to gather into small groups to gripe about what they think the Church in their area should be doing or not doing, or picket pastors or bishops to the same end because there is no effective, visible, established forum for expressing and resolving these matters within the Church.

A few bishops have already mandated parish and diocesan councils and have spelled out their structure and functions. The attitude of most bishops, however, seems to be that if councils are that good they will develop spontaneously. They will not. Councils in the United States will not issue full-blown and successfully operable from the brow of the apostolic delegate, the ranking cardinal, the executive director of the National Council of Catholic Men or anyone else. They will require a long and arduous peroid of trial and error in learning how to work in groups, experiencing frustration and failure, but patiently and prayerfully starting again.

They will not gain this necessary experience if they do not get started. For that, the leadership of the bishops, in view of the nature of the Church, is required. Mandate may well be inadvisable because it may lead to poorly understood, ineffective paper councils. But strong encouragement and some initiative on the part of the bishops is essential. The responsibility of the rest of us is to encourage the bishops to establish the councils, and then to respond generously with our time and talents.

Whether a bishop acts by mandate or by invitation, he must make clear that he wants the councils and that he will assume his proper role in them. He should indicate that councils are not to be an extension of his or the pastor's rule or control, or a rubber stamp of his or their policies and decisions, but rather that they are to be forums for developing facts and insights from the whole local Church, including the bishop and the pastors. He should describe the councils as vehicles by which communication down will be supplanted by communication around and means by which authority will be powered by Christian love and the perceived truth of the matter, not by command, or threat or any kind of manipulation or maneuvering.

To be such vehicles and to enjoy credibility, the councils will have to be truly representative. It might well be prudent and timesaving for pastors and bishops to appoint the membership of the first parish and diocesan councils, but with two clearly announced tasks: to develop a procedure for nomination and election in due time of representatives of the priests, religious and laity who should be represented in order to achieve the greatest practicable involvement of the people of God; and to conduct an educational program concerning the purposes and functions of the councils so that the electorates are encouraged to put forward and vote intelligently for candidates who have suitable qualifications and representative status. It would be disastrous if because of the ignorance or apathy of the electorate a council were captured by a selfish and determined group which used it to impose un-Christian views and programs or to block Christian ones.

One device for extending involvement beyond the necessary limits of council membership is to establish council committees to handle the various areas of interest, such as education, finances and community affairs, and to enlist noncouncil members for the committees to the greatest feasible extent. In addition to conducting frequent open meetings, the councils should invite upon appropriate occasions the attendance and advices of experts, scholars and, hopefully, saints. They should give audience to persons having suggestions or questions. They should listen to the elderly, the young, the reactionary, the radical, the confused, the assured, the rich and especially the poor. In this way the councils would capture and digest the dialog between the old and the new and circulate the nourishing truth throughout the evergrowing and maturing Church.

As the councils themselves mature, they should come to decisions by consensus rather than by majority vote. Consensus is not necessarily unanimity; sometimes it is a temporarily agreed compromise, a middle way. Its development is sometimes a long and arduous process. It requires not only willingness but also courage to be open and honest, not shying away from confrontation but listening to others and presenting one's own views with civility. This is a process which develops self-knowledge and true humility. It avoids putting down or humiliating others, and resolves polarization around two or more positions into unity around one. It is a most valuable process these days, and one that particularly becomes a people of God.

Considering the nature of the Church, the councils cannot have complete freedom of decision in matters of faith and morals. They are subject to what in the political order we call "constitutionalism." In our political system no majority of voters, however large, may infringe upon the basic human rights. Our founding fathers fought a bloody revolution to obtain these rights and established a government and a system of jurisprudence to protect them. Without them, the United States would not be American. Similarly, basic Christian truth and justice must prevail over mere numbers of votes, or even consensus within particular councils to ensure that the Church remains Christian.

An important role of the hierarchy in the conciliar structure is to ensure the supremacy of the Christian Constitution. It is quite possible that on race relations, for instance, a majority of the laity in this diocese or that, or even in the country as a whole, would vote today for a less than Christian position. The bishops could not permit that to go down as the official position of the Church. Sometimes, therefore, the pastors and the bishops may have to do more than exercise strong leadership. When matters of faith and morals are involved, they may have to exercise a veto. To guard against erroneous vetos as well as against erroneous majorities, a procedure for reference, and a form of appeal to a higher council will surely develop. The Magisterium will remain supreme in matters of faith and morals. But presumably the Magisterium itself will be linked with the new communication system and decision-making structure and will receive the benefit of the insights supplied by the councils.

A conciliar structure does not threaten the hierarchy or lessen its role. It would strengthen leadership by making it more credible. It does not threaten associations of priests, religious, or laity, or any of the special apostolates within the Church, or any of the societies within the parish. It is not intended to supplant any of them. On the contrary, it is intended to be a vehicle through which their activities and good works can more effectively support and receive the support of the whole Church. The structures of these special groups, therefore, would remain independent and appropriate to their nature and purpose. But for the Church as a whole, except for appropriate bureaucracies, such as the Vatican Curia, the United States Catholic Conference, state Catholic conferences, and diocesan curias which operate as administrative arms of their own councils, no other structure will be needed. Its simplicity is startling. It is impossible to imagine a structure better designed to ensure the Church's credibility, adaptability and contemporary relevance.

Catholic Conferences and Bishops' Synods

A word might be said about the new organization plan of the United States Catholic Conference adopted in 1969 by the National Council of Catholic Bishops upon the recommendation of an outstanding management firm. The move was not a restructuring of the Church in the United States. It was a restructuring of the bureaucracy which takes care of the multitude of administrative housekeeping chores of the Church in the United States. The restructured bureaucracy remains firmly in the hands of the bishops. It is good to note that more laymen are to be involved in making the decisions, even though the laymen are selected by the bishops and their function is purely advisory.

At the moment, therefore, it is not clear whether the Conference has been updated to enable the bishops to serve the Church more effectively than its predecessor, the National Catholic Welfare Conference, or whether it is to enable the bishops to control the Church more effectively. The latter purpose may be prudent for the short term because of the present existential strains and confusions of drastic change. Viewed as a control mechanism, the reorganized Conference would provide strong leadership during a period of transition, train elements of the Church not heretofore involved in decision making, and thus guide the Church to the conciliar structure suggested by Vatican II. If this be the case, the Conference would ultimately become the administrative office of the United States Catholic Pastoral Council. (The bishops have in fact appointed a committee to study this possibility.) Precisely the same remarks apply to the several state Catholic conferences which now exist or are being formed.

A similar comment might be offered concerning the synod of bishops of the world meeting with the pope, the relationships that are developing between individual bishops and senates of priests within their dioceses and the much pressed proposal that associations of priests be admitted to direct discussions with bishops at national and Vatican synods. Such meetings are to be applauded, so long as their agendas are confined to matters of interest between the priests and their bishops alone. But on matters of broader scope, they would obviously extend the base of decision-making only one step. It would be an important step so far as the tapping of expertise is concerned, but a small one so far as membership of the people of God is concerned, and far from representative of all of the interests and problems of the Church. In any event, councils do not threaten the existence or proper purposes of priests' senates or associations. Indeed, they would assist in the achievement of their goals.

Necessary Amendments of Canon and Civil Laws

A conciliar structure may require changes not only in canon law but also in the civil laws of many states. Under both systems of laws it is doubtful that the function of the councils at the present time can be more than advisory. Canonists are presumably studying any needed changes in the Church's laws to give the councils appropriate authority. Some group (the United States Catholic Conference, the National Council of Catholic Men?) should be studying what changes are required in the laws of each state and then mount a program to obtain required amendments. Civil laws affect only the temporal affairs of the Church. But if councils are to act as well as to investigate and discuss, temporal affairs will inevitably be involved. Civil laws may have to be amended to provide the councils with authority and power to make legally enforceable commitments of a temporal nature. Exactly what authority and power should be given councils subject to what checks and balances to avoid the faults of trusteeism, will require wise and creative thought.

Aside from the matter of the legal status of councils, it is high time that the civil laws respecting the conduct of the temporal affairs of the Church in the United States be carefully checked. Most of these laws were passed around the turn of the century, usually at the behest of the bishops. The laws followed drafts prepared by their lawyers to reflect the bishops' understanding of a suitable accommodation of the needs of the Church as a religious society and the needs of the Church in temporalities. The history of trusteeism had considerable influence on the bishops' thinking as to what was suitable. These laws should be examined and, if necessary, updated to permit modern operations. It is not safe to ignore them, as is so often done today in deciding to do "the sensible thing." A "sensible" course of action adopted in a particular situation in a manner not strictly in accordance with the procedures prescribed by the law of the place might be blown out of the water in an injunction suit brought by some zealot or malcontent. Or a contractual commitment made in a similar cavalier fashion might be declared void, leaving someone personally exposed to serious financial loss or liability.

Examination of these laws should proceed from the point of view that in temporal affairs the bishop is trustee. This designation and the attendant powers and responsibilities have long been set forth in Church law, but there has been no effective provision for enforcement of those duties or remedies in event of their breach or neglect. Presenting a case through Washington to Rome, with at best only a "cease and desist" order as the possible outcome, is not an effective remedy. Recognition under state laws of the powers and responsibilities of bishop as trustee in the temporal affairs of the local Church to the same extent as those of a trustee of other temporal trusts is indirectly suggested in the laws of many states. It should be made explicit. This simple clarification, incidentally, might solve the problem receiving so much comment in the Church these days about the desirability of complete financial reporting. There would be a clearly defined legal path to enforce that normal trusteeship responsibility.

Just as the bishops led the enactment of the present state laws, so now they should lead the enactment of updating amendments. Furthermore, they should have their lawyers check such documents as the articles of incorporation and bylaws of institutions, especially parishes, which they have established to be sure they conform to the letter and the spirit of the existing laws. They should also see to it that all concerned are instructed in these legal matters. In some dioceses, for instance, parishes are incorporated under state laws that require an annual or biennial meeting of the congregation for the election of lay trustees by the members of the parish. Not only is there notable indifference toward the regular holding of such meetings, but members are often by practice and sometimes by by-laws restricted to adult male members. Disfranchisement of adult female members is not only an outdated attitude; it is legally dangerous.

Every bishop should be aware that failure to update statutes and practices invites civil suits seeking to find common law remedies, if not statutory provisions, to enforce the obligations of the bishop as trustee, or to upset contractual commitments for, say, the building of a church, the installation of a new organ, or simply to bring to the attention of the world that the Catholic Church, strong on law and order in most respects, is sometimes careless about obeying laws directed toward its own conduct.

Reasonably Effective Councils Now

Pending any needed amendments of state laws, there will be problems of adapting councils to the present structures recognized by those laws. An important example is the boards of trustees or directors who now manage parish affairs in many dioceses. These officials should be ex officio members of their parish council and should dot the legal i's and cross the legal t's in accordance with the moral authority of their council. Adaptive arrangements such as this can almost always be worked out. There is no need to await the amendment of state laws before establishing councils. Even if the legal status of the councils is purely advisory, that is sufficient during the learning period required to make the Council system effective. Despite the foreseeable difficulties that will be encountered in establishing the councils and getting them to operate effectively, the start should be made. The perfect is often the enemy of the good, and too much good is at stake here to justify unwillingness to suffer error in trial.

The councils will end the era of mounting hobby horses and rocking off in all directions. They will do much to end the agony of role confusion and identity crises. They will assure that the Church will never again lag in relevant responses to change. Through them the people of God with dignity, reason, civility, humor, confidence, courage, faith and love will together decide upon both inward-directed and outward-directed Christian action. Injustice in the Church cannot survive such a system. The very method of arriving at decisions as well as the resulting actions will make the presence of Christ in the world credible—to all mankind, but not least to the members of the household of the faith who are suffering most in this period of great change.

Wittingly or unwittingly, councils are one of the most radical suggestions of Vatican II. (Judging from the lack of implementation by most of the bishops when they got home, perhaps the suggestion of councils was put over on the bishops by the Holy Spirit.) If the concepts of purpose, function and makeup of councils suggested by the bishops are implemented, the entire people of God will be involved in developing the nature, purpose and action of the Church of the future.

A fully developed conciliar structure from parish through diocese and nation to continent and the Vatican itself will move the pilgrim Church on its way as fast as the people of God are prepared to move it. This movement may be rapid, it may be slow, but it will be certain. The Church will move, and its progress will be authentic and highly visible all the way.

As each person and each group of people is influenced by and changed by all of the psychological and physical forces in the environment, the Church will change because of the direct immediate leverage on it provided to and applied by the people.

The Church will no longer seem to be "they," because it will no longer operate as "they," or to all appearances, only by and through the hierarchy. The Church will become "we," all of the People, including the hierarchy, because it will operate that way. The Church will become existentially and factually, not just theoretically and theologically, what the people of God become, without any slippage or masking.

What the people of God, the Church, will become is beside this point, and in any event unpredictable. Our faith that Christ and the Holy Spirit are with us until the end of time is, however, solid ground for hope and confidence that the Church will become the creative force, the light of nations it was established to be.

This faith and confidence in the guidance of God relieves the people of God of no responsibility, nor does it ensure that they will in all cases, or with sufficient speed, meet their responsibility. Indeed, they may from time to time wander in the desert and may even worship golden calves. The point remains for better or for worse, the Church will become precisely what the people of God become. There is assurance that after any wandering in the desert or worshiping of false idols God will lead his people to holiness again.

In explaining the nature of the Church, apologists will no longer resort to such euphemisms as the "hidden," the "mystical," the "real" Church. They will define the Church by what it is, a pilgrim people, even a sinful people with most of whom God may not be well pleased at any given time. As in everything else in creation, its nature will be determined and defined by what it does, not by what its members do as individuals but what they do as a people. How it does what it does, and particularly how it comes to decisions about what to do, will be recognized as critical components of what it does.

The people of God will need preachers and teachers as never before. There will have to be men of wisdom, holiness and courage who will constantly confront the pilgrim people with the word of God and will require them to return to those fundamental principles without which the Church is not Christian and the people are not people of God. Hopefully, this role will be adequately filled by those to whom it was given as their primary responsibility—the clergy, from pope to simple priest.

The Church will develop like the Jews developed by responding to their holy men with greater or less understanding and good will in the changing environment in which they found themselves from century to century. There will be two notable differences: the pace of development will be much faster. It will match the increasing pace of development of the world of today and tomorrow compared with that of the millennia before Christ. And any possibility that a priestly caste may hinder development, change and growth will be minimized to negligibility. Under the council structure the role of hierarchy and priests will be that of servant leader, not master rulemaker.

The council idea is revolutionary. Its implementation, which is irreversibly underway, will be revolutionary in fact. The realization of Christian truths, values and ideals will be the work of all men under the guidance of the Holy Spirit. Let us pray that we will be open to his inspirations and responsive to his promptings.

Toward a Structure for Education

So much for the overall picture. We hope that no reader has become impatient or feels that this discussion is irrelevant to the question of a structure for Catholic education. The Church's educational system can be treated as a separate subject, and it must have its own appropriate organization. The Father, the Son and the Holy Spirit can be treated separately, too, and perhaps each has a function and a mode of acting peculiar to himself. But treatment by such a method results too easily in our forgetting that the three Persons are a community constituting one God. So, too, a treatment of the educational apostolate of the Church aside from the Church as a whole may have two unfortunate results. We may forget the fundamental purpose of Catholic education, and we may not provide a place for it in the overall structure of the Church.

A few reflections about the present situation may suggest the direction which restructuring of educational systems ought to take. There are two fundamental defects in the present system. It is not organized as a system, and decision-making is not broadly based. Both defects seem to be largely the result of the bishops' attitude toward education. They have either insisted upon, or have done nothing to change, the autonomous sink-or-swim-on-your-own-resources parish school, for instance. By that attitude the bishops have signalled that they have the exclusive right, without the obligation to consult anyone, to determine educational policy, including the policy of having no policy, no system. Their attitude seems to be that the school is their baseball. If they are not allowed to be pitcher, captain and coach of the team, that's just too bad. They will take their ball and go home, and there will be no game.

One official explanation of why Catholic school enrollment is dropping is that the schools are deliberately adjusting enrollment to effect better teacher-pupil ratios. Another is that religious vocations to teaching orders are shrinking and that parents cannot or will not contribute enough money to pay for lay teachers to fill the gap.

The honest position is not that the schools are deliberately adjusting enrollment. A better, and certainly desirable, teacher-pupil ratio is normally achieved simply by hiring teachers and by adding facilities to the extent necessary. No, enrollment is dropping because parents are withdrawing their children. They are not doing this for personal financial reasons. The enrollment drop is occurring almost entirely in the grade schools, and it started several years before any grade schools started to charge tuition. Even now most grade schools do not charge more than a nominal amount of tuition, if any. Enrollments in high schools are just beginning to drop a trifle, despite the fact that the high schools have always charged substantial tuition.

Parents are moving their children to the public schools for two related reasons. First, the parents believe their children receive a better or more comprehensive education there. Second, the parents have found it impossible to get the authorities to update the curriculum and improve the quality of education in the particular Catholic school their children have been attending. It adds up to an unsatisfactory present situation coupled with the fear that the future will see not only no improvement but no school.

When parents ask, as they have, the diocesan school authorities to show them a plan and the cost of improving the schools so that they may contribute their pledges of dollars, they are brushed off. Or they are told, "Have faith in the superintendent of schools," and are blandly shut out. Then in some corner of the diocesan newspaper they may read, "The pastor of the parish is the canonical principal of the school. The superintendent of schools can make suggestions to him but can enforce no rules or standards." They suspect that this official line is designed to excuse the superintendent or the bishop from doing anything effective about the schools. But there it is, and there it lies. They can find no canon lawyer in the diocese who knows, or is willing to say, whether the official line is correct or not. So their frustration becomes complete.

Instead of devising and presenting a visible and viable school system which the Catholic community might well be led to support on a voluntary basis, the powers that be, plus many good people who have given up on the powers that be but sincerely want to preserve the schools, resort to the taxing power of the state. Unfortunately, the latter group fails to realize that lack of money is not the root of the problem and that obtaining money from the state might actually aggravate the problem.

Two things could result from resort to public aid. First, the campaigns for public funds could fail. In that case the Catholic community, having been persuaded by their bishops and school authorities that they cannot support the schools themselves, will not do so, and the schools will be closed one by one. Second, if the campaigns should succeed, there would be even less pressure to improve the schools. The pressure from the competition of the public schools would be relieved. The pressure from parents to improve educational quality could be disregarded. Worst of all (as will be explained in the next chapter of this book), aid would be given only to the extent that the schools became secularized like the public schools. For all practical purposes, the Catholic schools would become branches of a system which is constitutionally prohibited from adding a sectarian or spiritual dimension to what is taught. So, despite the good people who administer and teach in them, public schools are materialistic and secularistic.

Strong Leadership vs. Exclusive Control

The bishops insist, especially when a case involving the right of the Catholic schools to exist reaches a Supreme Court, that the education of a child is a God-given parental right which the state must honor and protect. At no time do they leave any doubt that the responsibility for financing the schools is the laity's, either alone or with the help of anyone else whose assistance they can obtain by persuasion or by force of law.

Yet the bishops keep an exclusive grip on the administration of the schools. Laymen may hang their clothes on the hickory limb of advisory parish and diocesan school boards, but they may not go near the water of policy making, administration, cost information and financing methods. The schools will not survive this style of mortmain. Decisions with respect to Catholic education must be more broadly based. Principles of participative management under the leadership of the bishops and subject to their control in matters of faith and morals must be instituted.

By the nature of the apostolate and by virtue of their office, the bishops must lead in the solution of the education problem. If there is any one question that justifies preoccupation at the present time, it is education. Controversies about vocations, celibacy, birth control and other matters concerning the institutional Church can be left for a while to God if necessary. But only we can create and maintain a good educational system. If we do not do so, we will be within a generation a people of superficial Christianity at best. We can even leave the present generation of adults to God. But we would be shirking our duty if we left the children to Him. However, it is not likely that we will be confronted with any such either-or choices. It is the bishops' responsibility to provide effective leadership in this cause, but they have not given such leadership in the last few critical years.

Take the bishops' 1967 Statement on Catholic Education. The Statement contained many pluses and some serious minuses. The bishops are "for" the schools as "an indispensable component of the Church's total commitment to education in the United States." There is recognition in this phrase of the civic as well as the religious responsibility of the schools. The Statement is not triumphal about the successes of the schools in the past with respect to either responsibility. It calls for research—by someone not specified or suggested—to help determine how the schools may be improved and how adequate financing may be achieved.

The whole document is low key—too low key. It mentions weariness, discouragement, widespread concern about inability to provide sufficient funds for all of the Church's educational institutions and programs. But it contains no suggestions as to how these are to be overcome. There is merely a plea for confidence and the promise that the bishops will do their part. What part the bishops conceive to be theirs is not indicated. However, the role to be played by the teachers is well spelled out and by implication so is some of the part to be played by the laity. There are, for example, the excellent suggestions that the teachers should get involved with home and school associations, school boards, parish councils, associates in the public school sector and local organizations endeavoring to improve the environment of the young. Since all of these groups are largely lay groups, a call to the laity to form and participate in them seems logical.

All of this is great—great. So what is missing? Well, perhaps one of the teachers to whom the Statement is largely addressed might say: "This broad description of the dignity, the importance, and the opportunities of the vocation of a Catholic school teacher is splendid, but I know all that. What I want to know is whether there are going to be any Catholic schools to teach in until my retirement age and whether there is any use in my encouraging vocations to a religious teaching order."

The bishops' Statement contains no answers to this fundamental question. It is just a request for confidence that the present uncertainties will pass and reliance upon time and the Holy Spirit to solve the problems. (The reference to a three-year research program—which has not been heard of since—has all of the encouragement to action of a parliamentary motion to lay the matter on the table or to postpone it indefinitely.)

There is still little evidence that the bishops throughout the country have changed their attitude about criticism of the schools.

When parents and other concerned laity start asking about the schools in their area, the bishops insist that Catholic schools are as good as—nay, better than—the public schools. "Oh, there are a few exceptions here and there, but the superintendent of schools knows all about these weak spots and is taking steps to correct them. Everything is under control. Have complete faith in him." With such assertions the bishops completely shut out the questioners. There are no plans for updating curriculum, facilities or teacher qualifications and no evidence of interest in such planning. The laity sees no current budgets and no interest in using budgets for planning the future.

The fact that the sixth grade children in the Catholic schools of one city or state, or the tenth grade students in the Catholic schools in another city or state did better in certain standard tests than the national average, or even that, in general, Catholic school children do better than children generally does nothing to reassure parents concerned about the education of *their* children.

It is one thing for a bishop to ask for faith in the Trinity, in Christ or in the Church. It is presumptuous to ask for faith in one man's ability to supervise an educational system with all of the professional and administrative competences required. This is not a matter of faith in supernatural mysteries. It is a matter of confidence in natural human qualifications and the right to withhold confidence until the qualifications have been demonstrated.

What the Catholic community wants most at the present moment from each of its ordinaries with respect to the schools and the other educational programs of the diocese is a statement somewhat like this: "Here is a plan for our schools and our CCD programs for the immediate and foreseeable future. Here is what it will take in the way of resources. Here is what it will cost; here is the way we can handle it. If you don't understand it, or if you disagree with any part of it, let's hear from you. I am sure we can iron it out. I am suggesting a target date of six months for this process of publicity and discussion. Then I hope you will show your support of a comprehensive program by pledging your dollars." Such an approach by all of the bishops would give the laity confidence that Catholic education has a future.

Unfortunately, nothing in the bishops' Statement, and nothing they have said or done since its issuance, gives any inkling that the bishops as a whole appreciate the desirability of such an approach. Perhaps their reference to research into needs and resources is a start toward beginning to think about planning to plan. Certainly research of that type is long past due, and it is vital for long-range planning. But to offer research instead of a positive program to meet presently known needs and to tap presently visible resources is like shouting to a drowning man to tread water because you are going to throw him a book on the buoyancy properties of water as soon as you can run back to your library and get it. It almost seems fair to characterize the Statement by a line from Gilbert and Sullivan: "Mere corroborative detail, intended to give artistic verisimilitude to an otherwise bald and unconvincing narrative."

Centralized and Participative Management

But let us turn from criticism, set aside the St. Catherine of Siena role and look at some practical suggestions for restructuring the educational system so that it may have a future. The key words are "central" and "participative."

All studies and thinking on restructuring point to the need for central planning, central administration, central purchasing and central financing. The problem is how to centralize. What matters should be centralized? At what level should each of them be centralized? In what hands should centralization be placed? These are not easy questions to answer, and an answer that fits one section of the country might not fit another. For example, methods that would fit a diocesan corporation might not fit parish-by-parish corporations.

It would be most helpful at this time of crisis to establish a system of communication among the many groups working on the problems, so that the ideas, successes and failures of established systems quickly became common property. Is there some spirit of competition or rugged individualism that prevents this, or are we just too lazy to devise the mechanics? Perhaps the United States Catholic Conference or the National Catholic Educational Association could set up a clearing house for the current and comprehensive dissemination of such information, and give widespread publicity as to its availability.

Another thing needed is a study of canon law and of the laws of each state to determine the boundaries within which centralization may legally move, or to determine in what respects canon law and state laws should be amended to permit effective centralization. The need for such a study, and the probable need to amend these laws in connection with overall Church structures has already been given considerable attention in this chapter.

As stated earlier, the suggestion that canon law as presently interpreted might forbid centralization of educational matters in a parish-by-parish corporation situation is shocking. If it be true, many of us will be stopped cold in our efforts to organize our present non-system into a system, but we had better realize it and make the proper efforts to get canon law changed or interpreted more liberally before counting ourselves dead. As to state laws, studies are almost certain to disclose the need for amendments to legalize the many temporal aspects involved in centralization.

Meanwhile, recognizing the need to conform practices to existing canon and civil laws, let us look at one example of what might be done to accomplish centralization. One archdiocese has been studying the feasibility of deeding all grade and high schools in its several dioceses to a single corporation to be operated thereafter by that corporation. All new schools in the archdiocese would be built and similarly owned and operated by the corporation. Curriculum, teacher qualifications, salaries, hiring and all major policies for the schools would be determined by the corporation through its board of directors and its administrative staff. Although several of the board members would be appointed by the ordinaries in the archdiocese, most of them would be elected by the laity. The corporation's commitment to the doctrines of the Catholic faith would be ensured by its articles of incorporation. The corporation would assess each parish or each group of parishes which has a school according to their ability to pay. The corporation would conduct diocesan drives for additional funds, if needed. This is a corporation sole situation which has a tradition of conducting other activities on a centralized basis, so no serious canon or civil law problems seem to be present.

Some psychological factors in that plan could have serious practical effects. For instance, the scheme does not seem to have enough home-rule aspects to keep parishioners interested in either the excellence of their school or in contributing to the parish's assessment for it. Interest in both of these matters is of the greatest practical importance but might be lost if the local parishioners came to feel that "city hall" or "they" were running the school with little or no local involvement or responsibility. In a noncorporation sole situation, where the individual parishes own their own churches and schools, it might be difficult to persuade the parishes to deed their schools outright to a central corporation.

To meet both of these practical objections, there might be a sale and lease-back arrangement, modelled upon those commonly used in business. In a parish-by-parish corporation situation, the parishes would deed their school properties to a central corporation and lease them back for a rent, adjustable from time to time in accordance with ability to pay. The lease agreements would place on the parish the responsibility for running the school, subject to meeting standards set by the diocesan board of education. The lease agreements would also give the parishes the right to recover the school properties from the corporation in order to protect their investment if the school should ever be discontinued.

In a corporation sole situation, since the school properties are owned by the diocese rather than by the parishes, the initial sale to the new corporation would be by the diocese, and the corporation would lease the premises back to the individual parishes. The advantage of a sale and lease-back device is that it establishes a relationship between a central agency and a given school whereby centrally established standards become legally enforceable obligations. Yet original ownership rights are protected.

Although I do not favor the foregoing devices, I have described them at length because many dioceses are considering incorporation of the central agency which they have concluded is desirable. The heart of the matter is the existence of a central agency having authority to fix and administer standards for all of the schools. These standards should not be inflexible, but they should require at least minimum qualifications for each program and flexibility among them to permit experimentation under professionally competent supervision. Once established, that agency could perform all necessary administrative functions to achieve an effective educational program without the need of formal, legally enforceable ties with the educational units it serves. The relationship should have built-in incentives to local interest and support, with emphasis on service to them, not impersonal stand-offish controls.

Central administration must be something more, something better than a mechanical, legalistic structure. It is a people structure, and it will succeed or fail on the basis of the understanding, good will and voluntary cooperation of those engaged in its activities, not upon contractual provisions. It embraces everyone involved in Catholic education and all of the relationships between them: the bishop, the superintendent of education and his staff, the superiors of the teaching orders of sisters and brothers, the parish priests, the principals of the schools, the CCD and the Newman apostolate directors, the school and CCD teachers both religious and lay and the parents of the children. In the past this would have completed the list. In the future the list will have to be extended to include the entire Catholic community, probably through representatives serving on parish and diocesan councils or boards of education. Finally, the list will have to be extended to include the counterparts of all these persons in the civic community for the Church will recognize how important and necessary are close relationships between the public and the private sectors of education.

Central administration is ultimately an organizational problem, but while we are renovating and streamlining the structure it will be a communications problem of the first water. It is gratifying to read of the work that has already been done in a number of dioceses. Some have boldly updated structures. Others have established groups comprised of clergy, religious and lay people to study the best methods of restructuring. We hope that these groups will not go it alone but will draw upon the experience gained by others and the expertise of the pros in the education department of the United States Catholic Conference and the National Catholic Education Association.

Hopefully, enough laymen willing to commit their talents to the difficult patient work that will be required will offer their help.

Changes in Religious Orders Affect Catholic Schools

It is beyond the scope of this book to discuss particular structures, such as one for a grade school, a high school, a CCD program or a college. Such structures now exist, and if a particular one is not functioning well, the personnel involved undoubtedly know, or are being told, of its shortcomings. Presumably, they are sufficiently competent to make adjustments dictated by changing requirements and conditions.

However, one development with respect to colleges should be mentioned. It is closely allied with the ecumenical movement and may well be spurred by the remarkable directive issued on April 1, 1970, by the Secretariate for Promoting Christian Unity with the approval of Pope Paul. This document strongly urged cooperation and collaboration among institutions of higher learning operated under not only Catholic but also other Christian auspices. The directive set forth guidelines for the pursuit of studies of theology, and indeed of all academic subjects. Several such arrangements are being tested. Some involve one college's moving to the campus of another. Some involve cooperation among several colleges (Catholic and Protestant, men's, women's and co-ed) whereby faculty and students are exchanged and special facilities are shared. At least one group is studying the setup and experience of such institutions as the Universities of Toronto, Cambridge and Oxford to determine whether in an American setting a number of colleges, while retaining their individual character and purpose, could operate under a central body. The latter might not constitute a university but would at least provide general administrative services to all. Such arrangements might prove the salvation of many colleges by enabling them to offer broader educational opportunities at competitive costs.

Particular structures for groups related to Catholic education are beyond the scope of this book. Several brief but important comments, however, should be made about them.

Some teaching orders of men and women religious own schools and colleges and are rethinking the advisability of continuing such ownership. They have recently been startled by a scholarly thesis which holds that under present legal setups the orders do not really own any educational institutions which they may have incorporated under state law; instead, the public owns them.

The publication of the thesis served a most useful purpose in that it brought to the attention of religious orders many considerations of legal and moral responsibilities that may have escaped their notice in the past. For example, accounting systems must be maintained accurately for both the order and the incorporated institution because the two are separate legal entities.

But the thesis went further. It contended that a religious order which establishes a separate corporation to own and operate a high school or college or hospital and spins off to it certain assets with which to operate has permanently dedicated those assets to a public educational or charitable purpose. If the order should sell the institution and liquidate and dissolve the corporation, the assets it receives may not be freely used by the order for its own purposes (such as caring for its older members) but must apply the assets to some *public* educational or charitable purpose.

This is a new field of law. While I hope and believe that the thesis has been pushed to an unwarranted extreme, every religious order which has established such a corporation, or plans to do so, should retain a good lawyer to do two things: first, put into the articles of incorporation a dissolution clause giving the order the right to the net assets upon dissolution and liquidation, with the greatest freedom possible under the laws of the state to use or dispose of the assets; second, guide the order, with the assistance of a good accountant, to set up the item of "contributed services" on the books not as "contributed services" but as a deferred compensation obligation, so that at some time—at least upon dissolution and liquidation of the corporation—the accumulated amount will be paid to the order as a debt before "net assets" are determined, and thus be free and clear of any trust in favor of the public.

There are more pressing structural problems confronting religious orders. For example, some orders which operate educational institutions share with their counterparts in the public sector of education student pressures for some voice in everything from administration and house rules to teacher qualifications and curriculum.

The teaching orders also have their own structural problems, relating chiefly to two questions: how can they give more freedom to individual members and thereby achieve better community spirit and action; how can they finance the education of their members and the support of their disabled or retired members on an apparently shrinking base of active members? The problem of how ultimately to recover the value of contributed services which helped to build up schools and colleges, as well as hospitals and other public service institutions owned by religious orders, is just being recognized and posed to lawyers and accountants.

Other efforts to solve these problems will have important implications for Catholic education. It may result, for instance, in religious teachers being allowed to select their teaching location, or being hired solely on the basis of personal qualifications, instead of being assigned by superiors. Such a change could result in something other than uniform salaries for religious teachers. We hope that it will not be carried to such an extreme that it will result in inequitable or unbalanced distribution of available religous teachers among the schools, CCD programs and other desirable educational apostolates. There certainly will be new relationships between religious and lay teachers and administrators in all educational institutions. Decisions on residence rules will have a bearing on the need for the traditional parish convent. It is already time for parishes with empty or partly occupied convents to press the orders for a change in their rules which would permit the parish to rent the unoccupied space to members of other religious orders or even to certain classes of lay people, such as teachers, the elderly and the poor.

Finally, centralized administration of schools will, or should, involve schools owned by religious orders. Most of these are high schools; some are still called "academies." Centralization should support these schools and coordinate their programs with the overall educational plans of the diocese. It would be disastrous if the devil's tail of professional jealousy or politics discouraged and deadened the spirit of innovation for which most of the major orders of teaching priests and religious have become famous and to which they remain valiantly dedicated.

Diocesan and Parish Boards of Education

Having taken this brief look at particular structures, let us return to our main concern, a central organization for Catholic education, and how it can fit into the overall Church structures discussed in the early part of this chapter.

There are already a considerable number of advisory parish school boards, or boards of education where CCD programs have also been undertaken, and there are some advisory regional structures within dioceses. There are even a few advisory diocesan boards of education. But what we are looking for is a central structure at the diocesan level with authority to plan, organize, coordinate, appraise results, and replan, reorganize and recoordinate all of the individual educational programs within the diocese as a continuing service and support to each other and to the Catholic community as a whole.

This concept of a diocesan central structure, which the School Superintendents' Committee on Policy and Administration of the National Catholic Educational Association submitted in 1967, will be elaborated in the following pages.

There would be established in each diocese: a representative board of education with full policy-making authority to establish, expand (or consolidate or discontinue) and maintain all educational programs, including schools, CCD programs for both children and adults, Newman apostolates, programs for the disadvantaged and experimental projects.

This board would also develop and continue updating of mandatory minimum standards for all programs, with respect to facilities, including specifications of the kind and location of all schools, CCD projects and Newman apostolates, and specifications for facilities that may be used in common by schools and CCD projects.

In addition, the Board would set up curricula, including courses for special groups and experimental projects. They would estab-

lish the qualifications and salary scales for teachers, principals
or directors and key administrative personnel and would decide
upon methods of financing, including setting rates of tuition or
parish assessments, if any, for schools and CCD projects.

A diocesan office of education, headed by a superintendent of
education would have separate departments for the schools, the
CCD programs, etc., each headed by an assistant superintendent
or director.

The superintendent and his assistants would administer the policies
and standards set by the board of education and would provide
professional counsel and supervision to all educational units, including experimental projects. They would plan for and to the greatest
practicable extent handle or direct central or regional recruiting for
all educational units of teachers, principals, directors and administrative staff, both religious and lay. This function would include
hiring specialists, such as speech therapists, to serve throughout the
school system. They would also make arrangements with the
religious teaching orders for balanced and equitable assignment of
teachers throughout the entire educational system.

The superintendent and his staff would supervise the purchasing
of textbooks, educational aids and materials, furniture, furnishings
and supplies, including possible TV facilities.

Architectural services, building sites and construction, insurance,
or funding for self-insurance, and personnel benefit programs would
be contracted for through the office of the superintendent. He
would also develop and enforce a uniform cost-accounting system
for all schools, CCD projects, Newman apostolates, and special
educational programs, and would develop and furnish the board of
education with information and recommendations, including annual
budgets, financial statements and long-range plans.

Every three to five years the superintendent would conduct a
parish-by-parish survey of foreseeable needs and resources for
schools and CCD programs, and he would establish and maintain
liaison with other diocesan offices of education and with all public
offices of education within the diocese to exchange information
about enrollments, curricula, methods, other matters of common
interest or matters that might affect each other's planning. The

superintendent would enlarge the staff and facilities of the office of education when and to the extent necessary to get the foregoing work done efficiently.

In a word, each diocese would have a representative policy-making board of education and an administrative office of education as vehicles to meet needs and solve problems for all Catholic educational programs except Catholic universities and colleges, but including Newman-type apostolates. There would be a diocesan annual fund drive for supplementary aid to parishes and for expenses of the board and office of education.

The board should be representative for the same reason that the Councils discussed earlier should be representative. Priests, religious and laity should be members, and the bishop or his representative, perhaps a vicar-general, should preside at meetings.

When the board is first established, the bishop might appoint members to avoid the delay of an election. Appointing members by the bishop might also be a good policy in the beginning because neither voters nor potential candidates would know the issues or the qualifications for members. The notion of a board or of a council is new, and there has been little experience in the country upon which to base an informational campaign to instruct the diocesan electorate.

Whether the first board is elected or appointed, its first assignment should be the development of a method for electing its successors. Priests should elect the priest members, religious the religious members and the laity the lay members, just as they do for councils.

Not only should the diocesan office of education, which is the administrative staff or bureaucracy of the system, be subject to board-established policy, but the head of that office, the superintendent of education, should be appointed by the board and serve for a term of office fixed by it. This post is akin to that of the president of a corporation. Professional competence in pedagogy would be useful, but professional competence in educational administration is the prime requirement of this position. The system will have great difficulty rising in excellence higher than the vision, courage and professional ability of this man.

A number of dioceses throughout the country have established committees or task forces to study the educational situation and to recommend what should be done. They are finding out that the situation is much as has been described in this book. It ranges from confused to chaotic. It may be necessary to suffer the delay of going through such studies because many persons have a vested interest in justifying the status quo and need to be really shaken before they will admit that the status quo is one of crisis. They are like the well-known mule which had to be clouted on the head with a two-by-four before it would move. Others feel that complete documentation, with all of the i's dotted and t's crossed, will be necessary to convince those to whom the report will be submitted that the situation absolutely, positively, with no if's, and's or but's, must be corrected.

If the committees and task forces do not unanimously recommend authoritative diocesan boards of education, they will have wasted their time and considerable sums of money. Their studies are precisely the kind of work a board of education should be doing constantly as a matter of course. In a deteriorating situation it would save time to establish the board immediately, let it dig out the statistical pieces, fit them together and go on from there. At very least, the board would prevent schools from closing haphazardly, as they now are. In the most pessimistic view, the board would preside (in Winston Churchill's phrase) over the orderly dissolution of the great school empire—a function which in reality is the only guarantor of the preservation of that empire. If after task force studies have been completed a board of education is not established, we can safely predict that another task force to make another study will have to be set up within two years. This will continue for about ten years at which time there will be nothing to study and report on except how to make the best deal for the sale of a few remaining school buildings.

A diocesan board of education should not take a modest, humble, meek view of its position. Zealous, aggressive, professionally competent management of the educational organization is called for. This will in many cases require enlargement of the staff of the office of education. Failure to do so because of a false sense of economy would be a gross disservice to the Catholic community.

Growth and modernization, and organizing for growth and

modernization, will require money—lots of it. This is not a matter for panic. The amounts required, as shown in the final chapter of this book, are no larger as a proportion of our resources than before. The money is available, but it is not wholly obtainable from traditional sources or by older methods. Hence, concurrently with modernizing the administration, the diocesan board of education should modernize the methods of raising and distributing the necessary funds. "Necessary" means sufficient to permit taking advantage of the best market conditions, but with the conviction that it does not pay to skimp on quality, whether of personnel or of materials, and that a competitive price for quality should be paid willingly.

We noted earlier that "systematize" and "centralize" carry the unpleasant connotation of "bureaucratize" and "institutionalize," meaning "fossilize." However, the latter is not the necessary result of the former. At a certain point in the development of size and complexity of social and economic organizations centralization and systematization must take place because, despite all the risks, there would otherwise be injustice, inequality and disorder. The wealthy parish, for instance, may sing the praises of autonomy. But the poor parish, with only its own limited resources, which tries to compete for teachers, for example, has the same delightful freedom as the poor man who is as free as the king to sleep each night under the bridge.

Under present canon law or civil law or both, one parish may not be required to contribute to another parish or to any cause other than its own needs. But neither canon law nor civil law has nullified the virtue of charity. Neither law prevents a bishop from seeking contributions from individual members of the Catholic community for stated educational purposes, including supplementary aid to poor parishes for their educational programs. Nor does any law prevent a bishop from using the parishes as solicitation centers for education funds with suggested contribution targets or quotas just as he now does for charities and other diocesan purposes. These would simply be charitable contributions to the bishop and from the bishop. There is no law against this. But perhaps there is fear of separating the men from the boys, the Christian Catholics from the cultural Catholics, fear of confronting the people in the pews with Christ's hardest saying, "You shall love your neighbor as yourself" (Mk. 12:31).

Once diocesan boards of education are organized and their members have become acquainted with each other and have begun to understand the problems of their diocese and have gained confidence in their ability to handle them, they should devote the greater part of their time and attention to formulating general objectives and specific goals, such as:

Objective

Ninety percent of Catholic children of grade and high school age in excellent Catholic grade and high schools within forty years. (One hundred percent is an unrealistic objective; 80%, or even less, might be more realistic in some rural or mountain areas. Thirty years might be a practicable target in some areas, fifty years in others.) In the meantime, an effective CCD program for all Catholic children not in Catholic schools and for adults.

Goals

1. Overall excellence of facilities, teachers, and curricula, in the schools and in CCD and other programs;
2. Equality of excellence among individual schools;
3. All schools (except privately owned ones) tuition-free (except to nonmembers of the Catholic community).

To complete the structure, below the diocesan board of education there should be parish boards of education. There might well be intermediate boards designed to handle and coordinate matters peculiar to particular areas, such as a particular metropolitan area or a particular rural area. Above diocesan boards might be a national board, and again possible intermediate boards for provinces or other convenient functional areas.

Questions and problems would be generated in the parishes which would have the primary responsibility for the elementary schools. Answers and services would be provided from the closest appropriate higher level. An important function of the levels above the parishes would be to help the parishes to see that the high school or high schools were theirs, not the property of some anonymous and autonomous group.

The boards of education should automatically match the parish, diocesan, national and possible intermediate councils described earlier. Since the councils will deal with all of the concerns and activities of the Church, each board of education should be an integral part of its corresponding council, probably one of its committees. Since education, whether by schools or by CCD programs or by both, involves the greatest need for expertise, common aims and cooperation in temporalities at both parish and diocesan levels, boards of education might well seek (even after their councils are established) their own type of members by elections separate from council elections. They may also conduct their business more formally than other council committees. In any event, the formation of boards of education should not be deferred pending the establishment of councils.

Implementing Christian Concepts

So many of the concepts of structure and management discussed in this chapter match those which modern business management has found to work that it does not seem out of order to suggest two other practical ideas from that source.

The profession of public relations has a bad name in some quarters, no doubt because the profession has been improperly used by some of its members and some of its clients to create a favorable image of a product or of a company which did not deserve it. But intelligent clients with long-range interests retain competent public relations men not only for image building but also for advising whether the desired image is deserved, and wherein their product, policies or activities should be improved to protect the image. Corporation managers who are intelligent enough to retain a public relations firm to provide this service are usually intelligent enough to consider seriously the advice they receive. They do not fire the public relations firm when it reports something they do not like to hear, or when it recommends a change which if adopted might be construed as a confession of the managers' ineptness or neglect or one that is likely to prove expensive. They have found that getting and following objective professional advice pays, even if the advice is painful.

Each bishop and the United States Catholic Conference, might well retain a good public relations firm to keep them informed of the actual image enjoyed by Catholic schools and CCD programs in the Catholic community and in the civic community, and then to help them respond effectively. A good public relations program is a highly effective type of research. Its feedback is sensitive and current.

Furthermore, when it comes to redefining and reselling the purpose and goals of Catholic education and to gaining the understanding and support of the faithful as a community, the bishops could do worse than employ good Christian public relations experts. Community fund organizations employ PR experts, and community funds constitute much the same type of effort discussed here.

The final practical suggestion is that for his next spiritual reading, each bishop should study a book or two on the role, functions and techniques of management—say, two of Peter F. Drucker's books on the subject.* The bishop should make the same suggestion to his superintendent of education and his top level school and CCD directors. And for their next spiritual retreat, let the bishops and these administrators take a week's course on the principles of management from a good business consultant. They should engage in dialog covering practical applications in the Catholic educational field. Such undertakings, religiously motivated and conscientiously pursued by the bishops and these administrators, could be of the greatest spiritual benefit to the bishops, the administrators and the entire people of God in these United States at this critical point in the Church's educational venture.

Within the last ten or fifteen years many of the largest corporations in this country and in Western Europe have adopted official

---

* *The Practice of Management* (New York: Harper & Row, 1954); *Managing for Results* (New York: Harper & Row, 1964).

statements of purpose and philosophies of management. They have unveiled and discussed them in conferences, sometimes in full-blown "advanced management" courses, with their executive and administrative personnel from mid-management level right up to the top. The documents are uncannily easy to read in terms of the goals of the Church and the selection and treatment of people for the performance of the Church's tasks.

No claim is made by corporations which have adopted such statements that they have completely succeeded in implementing them. Managers trained in the old school often find it difficult and sometimes impossible to turn themselves around. They "buy" the modern concepts but cannot wholly realign their reflexes. Neither can a great number of those whom they direct.

A similar lag in effectuating the new concepts of councils and of boards of education will be experienced in the Church. This is not grounds for discouragement. The new directions have been laid out by Vatican II. It has been declared in conciliar documents that the people of God, who are the Church, must have a clear concept of purpose and goals and must plan and act with intelligence and goodwill to achieve those purposes and goals under penalty of ultimate failure. The Church must also take into account the needs and talents of all its people—hierarchy, priests, religious and laity. It must also treat them justly in view of their total environment under penalty of their ultimate discouragement and failure.

Implicit in these declarations is the concept that the most powerful motivations of human beings are intangible, and they relate to the desire, not always consciously formulated, not only for well-being but for more-being. Man cannot live by bread alone. In business a philosophy of management designed without recognition of this truth is likely to leave a man with the feeling that he is in a rat race rather than a member of the good society in which he may work out a satisfying career. In the Church, a philosophy of structure which fails to take into account the dignity of man is likely to result in widespread loss of faith.

Donkeys are induced to move by carrots and whips. Men are motivated by material rewards or penalties, by necessity and adversity, by the desire to create, to conquer or to solve, and by the inspiration to renew the face of the earth and to improve the lot of their fellowmen. Even business has learned that men who possess the latter two motivations are likely to prove the best investment. How strange that the Church, which has always held these truths about men to have been revealed by God, should have been so long in perceiving their relevance to the activities of the Church itself.

But at long last we have the opportunity to apply these truths in practical fashion to the structure of the Church, and to the structure of its educational venture. When we have succeeded in doing so, daily pressures will be ameliorated by long-term vision; authority-push will be supplemented by service-pull; drive will be supplanted by leadership; and individual efforts will be synergized by cooperative, community action.

How can even God create a community in heaven out of people who did not at least try to create community on earth?

6. Providing Money

The earlier chapters of this book developed the thesis that the Church, as Church, should pursue its educational work more vigorously and extensively than ever before. We advocated that the elementary and secondary schools in particular should be maintained, improved and expanded.

The overall problem of doing this comes down to two things: structure and money.

To be sure, much hard thinking and planning must be done and difficult changes in textbooks, educational materials and pedagogical methods must be made. Some people may have to be reassigned and many additional ones enlisted. Education must have a modern structure. And it all comes down to money.

We will treat only financial matters pertaining to the usual educational apostolates undertaken by parishes and dioceses—the schools, CCD programs for children and adults and programs for young people on secular campuses. Catholic universities and colleges are outside that field. None of them rely upon the financial support of the Catholic community in the same way that the rest do. They are supported and seem destined to continue to be supported by tuition, by contributions from alumni, corporations, and other friends who appreciate the values the institutions are supplying and by direct and indirect governmental aid (tuition grants, research projects, experimental educational programs). Thus the financing of Catholic colleges and universities is of too limited interest to be treated in this book. And quite frankly, it is difficult to suggest how the Catholic community could assist these institutions without endangering their independence. The desirability of such independence was expressed earlier in this book.

Human and material resources will be found for all desirable educational ventures if enough money is found to pay competitive prices for them. Are additional buildings, equipment, teaching aids needed? Money will buy them. Are more qualified teachers and administrators necessary? As many would have to be found even if the Catholic schools were closed because the same children would then be in the public schools. Whether public schools of different communities or public and parochial schools within the same or different communities compete for personnel, salaries will rise until sufficient numbers of qualified people are attracted to fill the required positions. In the meantime even the public schools are in difficulty financing the rising cost of education. Is our task hopeless?

If we were to accept as valid the expressed attitude of the bishops of the United States during the last few years, the answer would be grim indeed. They have been telling us that we cannot do it without public aid.

The Possibility of Significant Public Aid

However deserved may be the reputation of the bishops as good administrators, they seem at first blush to be deplorably poor psychologists. Their support of efforts to obtain public aid for the Catholic schools is based upon claims of justice and the assumption that somehow a way around constitutional barriers to such aid can be found. But the fact that these efforts are being made in tones of desperation in a context of rising school costs is giving the Catholic community the idea that such aid is not only just and politically possible but that it is necessary for the survival of our schools. This combination of hope of help from others and fear of being unable to do the job ourselves is a dangerous psychological combination. It could paralyze our will even to maintain much less to improve and expand the schools so proudly built over the last century.

The important question, of course, is not whether the bishops are poor psychologists but whether they are right. If we cannot support our educational programs by ourselves, then surely we should seek help wherever we can find it. First, we should decide whether the schools are good not only for us but also for the general public. If we can get public aid on terms that will permit us to maintain our schools as we want them, namely, as religious schools, then we should work to get it. If our chances of getting public aid on these terms are reasonably good, then the bishops are not poor psychologists. They are dealing realistically and courageously with the facts of life.

We must wonder, however, what life they are examining—life in these United States, life in some foreign country, or in Utopia. Judging from their references to the systems in The Netherlands, West Germany, Great Britain, Canada and a number of other foreign nations as reasons why the United States, "the foremost democratic nation of them all," should provide public aid to religious schools, it would seem that they are not well-informed about the facts of life at home.

Constitutional Interpretations

The bishops seem unwilling to face the fact that we have constitutional provisions that prohibit public aid for any religious purpose. Even if they recognize the constitutional barriers, they seem to think that a breach in them can surely be found. This is not a realistic appraisal of the facts of life in the United States today or in the foreseeable future.

Most public money for education has been provided by the states and their local communities. Past and even proposed federal aid amounts to less than 8% of these appropriations. If federal aid should be voted by Congress to religious schools for anything other than bare incidental costs, there is hardly a doubt that it would be stricken down by the United States Supreme Court. Provisions for bus and book expenses and a few special projects—"categorical aids" for such purely secular purposes as lunches, remedial reading and experimental methods of teaching—have been approved. This is helpful, but it is hardly a make-or-break item of expense. Appropriations for buildings will be forever taboo. Maintenance costs and teachers' salaries might pass muster to the extent that they arise out of the teaching of "secular subjects."

The constitutional barriers to aid by the states are more formidable. The federal Constitution states merely: "Congress shall make no law respecting an establishment of religion, or prohibiting the free exercise thereof."

But state constitutions are more specific. The following is from one state constitution:

> The right of every man to worship Almighty God according to the dictates of his own conscience shall never be infringed; nor shall any man be compelled to attend, erect or support any place of worship, or to maintain any ministry against his consent; nor shall any control of, or interference with, the rights of conscience be permitted, or any preference be given by law to any religious establishments or modes of worship; nor shall any money be drawn from the Treasury for the benefit of religious societies, or religious or theological seminaries.*

The Supreme Court of that state as recently as 1962 declared that "seminary" meant "school" when that constitution was written and that even child welfare bus laws are unconstitutional. It stated specifically that "the First Amendment provision [of the United States Constitution which prohibits laws respecting an establishment of religion] *lends itself to more flexibility of interpretation than the provisions*" [*of the state constitution*].** (Emphasis added.) It also stated flatly that aid may not be given to religious schools even if the aid would result in an ultimate saving of money to the general public. How would you persuade that Court concerning that constitutional language that more significant aids to religious schools are constitutional? At the very least, some new theory and form of aid would have to be presented to it, since you could not expect the Court to directly overrule itself.

* Article 1, Sect. 18, *Constitution of the State of Wisconsin.*
** State ex rel Reynolds v. Nusbaum, 17 Wis. (2) 148, 115 NW (2) 761.

Most of the other states have identical or substantially similar provisions (so-called Blaine Amendment type provisions, based upon the Church-state separation language of Jefferson and Madison). It is not impossible, merely unlikely, that in the future those constitutions will be amended by popular vote to permit that more than, say, bussing or textbooks or such incidental "categorical aids" may be provided to religious schools; or that the United States Supreme Court will reverse itself on the federal school aid issue, much less apply its reversal so as to nullify the more restrictive provisions of the state constitutions.

The New "No Religion Is Religion" Theory

A word should be said about the two possibilities just mentioned to justify the judgment as to their unlikelihood. The two are closely related. If state constitutions were by some political miracle amended to permit more than incidental aid to the schools (such as for bussing and textbooks), the United States Supreme Court under its present interpretation of the First Amendment would be obliged to declare a state law providing such direct aid to be unconstitutional by virtue of the First Amendment, made applicable to the state by the Fourteenth Amendment. Thus no substantial state aid would be possible, even though the state constitution were amended to permit it.

There is a new theory abroad in the land, however, and some legal advisors to the bishops appear to hold out great hope for it. The theory is based upon a different definition of "religion" than has prevailed in the past. "Religion" under this definition is something broader but shallower than belief in God and sectarian or nonsectarian concepts of man's personal and social responsibilities stemming from the existence of God. "Religion" is merely one's philosophy of life, one's point of view about the meaning or lack of meaning of life and the universe, one's attitude toward God or no God, one's concept of self as a creature of God and, therefore, significant, or as a chance development of doubtful significance. Using this definition, the fact that religion according to the old definition is not taught in the public schools proves that religion according to the new definition is taught there. This is a "no policy is a policy" line of thought. "No religion" is "religion." Thus, if it is constitutional to teach this new type of "religion" in the public schools (and it must be, because, it is alleged, it is taught there), it is constitutional to teach the old type of "religion" in private schools. It is, therefore, discriminatory and unconstitutional to provide tax money for the public schools but not for religious ones, and state constitutions which deny public support for schools that teach the old type of religion are unconstitutional because they deny equal, nondiscriminatory treatment. So the new theory goes.

I predict that, although this type of reasoning may appeal to men schooled in Scholastic logic and equipped with the fine mental cutting tools of casuistry, it will have no appeal whatever to men of a more modern, matter-of-fact cast of mind who are wholly incapable of making the necessary semantic adjustments to declare that black is white.

Reference to the Scholastic tradition may be a bit unfair. Schooling in the Irish blarney tradition may be more accurate. The American Catholic Church derives more from the Irish than from the Scholastics. The Irish are past masters at making language suit their purposes. They learned the art the hard way. Blarney was originally not a form of flattery; it was a life-saving art. It was a sin, of course, to lie outright, but it was no sin to dissemble, equivocate or otherwise manipulate language so that it seemed to say one thing but meant another when what was at stake was one's life or the lives of loved ones. Not quite that much is at stake these days, at least in connection with Catholic education. Yet it may be easy for the American hierarchy, which is predominantly Irish, to persuade themselves that bread is necessary to life, that religious education is more important than bread since it leads to eternal life, and hence that blarney may be used to obtain and preserve it.

Now, to be sure, the public schools teach subjects from a purely secular point of view. But even if secularism is considered a religion, which it is not, the public schools do not teach secularism. They are merely neutral toward religion. Belief in pure secularism as a philosophy of life is certainly as much a constitutionally protected civil right as is belief in religion, but it is not religion as our Founding Fathers saw religion when they adopted the First Amendment. Are we now ready to persuade the Supreme Court that the concept of religion has been enlarged since then so that in today's wisdom it includes the opposite of religion as our forefathers used the word? We Catholics already have much to answer for in driving the public schools into neutrality toward religion. We mounted the first legal actions which resulted in religious truths and values being completely barred from the public schools. How can we now gracefully contend that the secularism we helped drive them into is still religion?

The "Child Welfare" and "Purchased Public Service" Theories

But let us move out of this dreamland and reenter the workaday world. Let us examine the proposals being made in state legislatures to achieve, under present constitutional provisions and interpretations, public aid for our schools. This is where the action is at the present time. Upon the success or failure of these proposals will depend the possibility of obtaining public aid in any significant amounts in the foreseeable future. If they succeed, the next question, apparently not yet foreseen, or not yet faced, will quickly appear: can our schools survive public aid? We will address both points.

Two basic types of proposals are being presented. They have essentially the same conditions. One proposal, based upon what is called the "child welfare" theory, provides that the parents of children in private (including religious) schools would be reimbursed the amount of tuition charged by the school, up to a designated maximum per child per year. Most proposals to date place this maximum at $50 per grade school pupil, $100 per high school pupil. These amounts equal about one-fifth of present costs (exclusive of construction and maintenance of buildings) of operating Catholic schools. This proposal is said to be modelled after the GI and other grants-in-aid for college education and thus constitutional. Distinctions between the two types of grants, relevant to the question of constitutionality, are not mentioned by proponents. For example, they do not mention the fact that GI grants are given directly to the student, not to aid any particular type of college, but to help the student attend any college of his choice. Public as well as private colleges charge tuition and attending them involves other substantial expense. Under the child welfare aid proposal, on the other hand, the grants are given to the parents upon their proving that they have first paid tuition for their child or children in a private school. Since public schools do not charge tuition, the purpose of aiding only the private schools, all but a handful of which are religious schools, is completely exposed.

The other proposal is based upon what is called the "purchased public service" theory. Under it, the $50 and $100 payments would be made directly to the schools. Proponents compare this system to paying hospitals, including hospitals under religious auspices, for the cost of care of indigent persons who are on public welfare. They do not distinguish between the purposes of the two types of institutions, even though this difference has a bearing on constitutionality. They overlook the fact that it is no part of a hospital's purpose or practice to teach religion, but that teaching religion is a religious school's sole reason for existence. (This is not to say that Catholic hospitals which practice their religion by, say, not allowing abortions under liberalized laws, will not be forced to secularize in situations where they are the only hospitals in the community. For this and other reasons the day of the Catholic hospital may be drawing to a close. But Catholic hospitals are not needed solely as Catholic institutions as Catholic schools are.)

The "Secular Subject" Compromise

Under both proposals, the amounts paid may not exceed the actual (state-audited) cost to the school of teaching "secular subjects," or under some proposals, a specified percentage of the salaries of teachers of "secular subjects." Thus, it is a form of "categorical aid." These subjects are usually limited by name. In one instance they may be listed as "mathematics, modern foreign languages, physical science and physical education." In another that list may be extended to include "reading, spelling, language arts, science (not just physical science), English, government, American history, industrial arts, domestic arts and business education." In no event may any cost related to the teaching of religion be reimbursed, whether for tuition under the child welfare theory or for reimbursable costs under the purchased public service theory.

This sounds quite acceptable to most Catholics if they ever hear about it. It must be acceptable to the bishops, since they are publicly backing the Citizens for Educational Freedom and similar organized pressure groups in their campaigns to have these proposals adopted by state legislatures throughout the country. (We use the term, "pressure group" in a nonpejorative sense.) They have been successful in five states so far, although the courts have not yet given a final ruling on the constitutionality of these proposals. Whatever can possibly be wrong with such schemes?

Nothing except that they could well mark the first phase in the death of the Catholic schools as religious schools. The advocates of these proposals have followed the advice of experts in constitutional law and based the payments on the cost, or rather part of the cost, of teaching "secular subjects." What they have chosen to ignore and have failed to explain to their fellow Catholics is that a "secular subject," to meet the constitutional test must be a subject from which all sectarian, spiritual or religious truths, values, insights, comments, approvals, criticisms or "atmosphere" have been eliminated. These subjects must be taught just as they are in the public schools, "straight," even with the same textbooks, or with textbooks approved by the public school authorities, except that the teacher may wear religious garb and the walls of the classroom may bear religious pictures and a crucifix. In a word, these subjects may not be permeated with religion and there may be no integration of the secular and the religious in their presentation.

This is the system that converted the Catholic and the Evangelical Lutheran confessional schools in Germany into Nazi schools for Hitler youth. It can't happen here? There are more subtle ways of teaching children paganism than teaching them the superiority of a race. There are more subtle ways of teaching racial superiority than teaching genocide. There are less direct ways of influencing educational content than by a dictator's decree. Just cut down or cut out appropriations, or threaten to do so as a legislature may do in backlashing a bishop's criticism for neglecting the poor. Aside from this kind of influence on educational content, the uncertainty of future legislative appropriations makes reliance upon substantial public aid a very risky thing.

How do you plan programs under that ever-present uncertainty? What do you do, if aid is reduced or cut off, to get the Catholic community to revitalize their financial support muscles grown flabby through disuse?

That highly practical point aside, to whatever extent a given Catholic school qualifies for public aid under these proposals, to that extent it is no longer a religious school. Today a Catholic school would be permitted to qualify for reimbursement directly, or through tuition reimbursed to the parents, for one-fifth of its costs by scrubbing religion out of one-fifth of the subjects in its curriculum. Advocates of these proposals admit that they are asking for only this fifth "in order to get the principle established." Tomorrow they will seek two-fifths, then three-fifths, then four-fifths. Long before that point is reached, the schools would not be different perceptibly or in fact from the public schools except that there would be a religion class of half an hour a day and there would still be a few religious garbs and holy pictures. The whole purpose of our schools would have been subverted. Those who have masterminded this compromise have apparently decided that it may be necessary to destroy our schools in order to save them. If the principle is established on these terms, we shall have been led like lemmings to the sea of unrelieved secularism despite the fact that we established our schools to protect our children from secularism.

There is no sense, of course, in overdoing this picture. If the proponents of these measures know when to stop and state clearly their intention to stop at that point so that reimbursement is sought for the costs of teaching only those subjects which are really not susceptible of significant permeation with religious truths or values, perhaps our schools could be preserved as religious schools. Examples of "safe" subjects would be elementary reading, writing, spelling, arithmetic, modern foreign languages and, less clearly, domestic arts, industrial crafts, secretarial and office equipment operating skills and physical training (not "physical education"). But when at the very outset permeation is abandoned in English literature, government, history, business education and, of all things, "science" (a term broad enough to include every science of man, society and man's environment), the purpose of the schools has already been seriously subverted, and a disturbing nonchalance or ignorance is evidenced concerning the exchange of our birthright for a mess of pottage. Whether Catholic education were killed by carelessness, inadvertence or design, it would be dead. We might end with education by Catholics, but not with Catholic education.

The Mess of Pottage—Public Aid

The table in Appendix A shows the mess of pottage we stand to receive in exchange for our birthright of freedom—religious schools. The vast majority of Catholics live in cities and states with a Catholic population of 30% or more, and few of them earn so little income that they do not pay income taxes to the federal government. Many of them, in addition, pay state income taxes based upon the federal model. The table is, therefore, conservative in its showing of the slim dollar advantage of public aid to most Catholics. It is almost inconceivable that the bishops, the school administrators and the leaders of the good people who are working so hard to persuade legislators to vote public aid are not aware of how little after-tax real net value public aid would be to the Catholic community.

Perhaps those who are advocating public aid know that it can be given constitutionally only on these destructive terms; or they may be tired or lacking in nerve. Maybe they are too worn-out and discouraged to tackle with vigor the hard work of making a system out of our nonsystem of schools and of striving to achieve educational excellence in all of our schools. Perhaps they are afraid to present the complete facts and to exert sales pressure to get the Catholic community as a whole to support the schools. These problems are tough and require the attention of men, many men, of tough mind and vigorous spirit.

It is certainly easier to blame the crisis in the schools simply on lack of money and to say to the Catholic community and the general public: "Unless we get substantial public aid we will have to close the schools, and then you will all be sorry." The temptation to rely upon that solution will be surmounted only by men whose faith is strong enough to support them through weariness and discouragement.

In making a pitch for public aid the advocates advance all the right premises. But their conclusion is a non sequitur. They are like some intellectuals who vividly describe the weaknesses and failures of the schools, but then instead of concluding that everyone interested, and especially everyone in responsible administrative positions, should do what is necessary to improve the schools, they advocate phasing them out. So, too, the Citizens for Educational Freedom and similar groups give no perceivable attention to the primacy—in time as well as in importance—of educational excellence which is a sine qua non not only for inducing Catholic community support but also for persuading responsible legislators to vote public aid.

Certainly, as these people say, parents should have the freedom to have their children educated in schools of their choice, schools which teach religious and moral values instead of unrelieved materialism and secularism. But they immediately compromise this principle, 20% as an opener. Certainly, it is in the national interest that there not be one monolithic school system which could be captured by secularists, chauvinists, racists, Communists, Fascists or what have you. So they take a chance on abandoning this safeguard, 20% to begin with. Certainly, a strong private school system in competition with the public school system is good for both systems. So they eliminate 20% of this competition, for a start. Certainly, if we cannot enlist the necessary support of the Catholic community, the schools will close and the cost to the general public will skyrocket. But we are members of the general public, and we would be obliged to pay our proportionate share of that extra cost.

We do have freedom to educate our children in our own schools, and we could foot the entire bill ourselves if we would, as will be shown presently. Our attitude should be one of self-respect and pride that we are supplying the values of a private religious school system to the nation. We should not grumble about the cost and insist upon our rights. Christ did not teach the cynical expression, "Good guys finish last." He taught His followers to give, not to demand, and to serve the world by love and sacrifice without expectation of material compensation whether it was owing in justice or not. Our campaigns for public aid may be morally justified. But we cannot pretend that they are a blazing witness to the letter or spirit of the Gospels.

It is amazing at first to observe that certain Catholic intellectuals who were once articulate about decrying Catholic schools as separate, different, and hence divisive, undemocratic and un-American are now advocating public aid for the schools.

Perhaps the timing of their switch is significant, coming as it does with the appearance of the "secular subject" theory developed to solve the constitutional problem. Perhaps they understand better than their more naive fellow religionists that the result would be recognition of the principle of nondifference which they advocate, and that the theory is a promising thrust toward making the Catholic schools a branch of the public school system. Our schools would be temporarily separate, but in all other essentials they would be similar, democratic, 100% American.

It is a pity that we do not listen, really listen, to what our non-Catholic neighbors say about our campaigns for public aid. At a public hearing on a bill to aid private schools a Lutheran minister expressed the attitude of his denomination toward the proposal. He drove straight to the heart of the matter. "Our schools," he said, "are built and maintained by us to teach religious values to our children. Every subject taught in them is taught as a religious subject. We will not, we cannot compromise our purpose in order to get a little money for our schools. Please God, we will never lose our faith to the point where we are unwilling to make the sacrifices necessary to keep them open."

There was a Christian. He was not facing lions in the Coliseum. He was facing other Christians considering a proposal to do him and his people a favor. Only money, not life, was being offered him. But he saw the same issue confronting him: compromise of his Christian faith. He was not asked to surrender doctrines, to be sure;

but he had to face the equally important choice of how to live them. What do most of us call him, and many others who oppose public aid for our schools? Bigots.

A bigot in our parlance is not merely a mean person who obstinately, blindly and unreasonably opposes our religious beliefs and practices. He is anyone who opposes us, period. We cannot understand that a person, a part of whose very religious belief is that the Catholic Church is the whore of Babylon, cannot in good conscience vote for the use of part of his tax dollars to support the Scarlet Lady. We are so convinced of our good citizenry, our just-like-everyone-elseness, that we forget the unpleasant incidents of history that prevent others from accepting the image we have constructed for ourselves in these respects. We think that a little ecumenism—see how broad-minded, nonmonolithic, honest and neighbor-loving we are—will compel others to drop their suspicions and love us back, right now.

We fail to see that the few cautiously controlled ecumenistic gestures we are making have done little to give more than wild hope to brothers outside our Church that they may some day be able to drop their suspicion that these gestures are merely maneuvers and that behind them is a fixed purpose to gain more favors, more control, more power for good old number one. We are deaf and blind to the concern of men of good conscience who see us mounting massive and expensive campaigns for tax relief, tax appropriations and other favors and immunities for ourselves but are silent and absent from the public forum when it comes to proposals to aid others, such as the poor, especially the black poor. We cannot understand why our public image does not match the image we have of ourselves. We say that our opponents must be bigots.

Our drive for public funds is at very least poorly timed. Some see it as a pure power play. Even as a matter of practical strategy much prior effort in changing the actualities behind the image others have of us is indicated. Unfortunately, the proponents of public aid are not waiting for this to be accomplished. They seem to be unaware that they have no power to rewrite history. They seem to have little patience to do what is necessary to ensure that a new chapter of authentic Christian action will be written.

Not enough of us have asked proponents of public aid the direct question: "What about this secular subject condition? Does it really mean that English literature, biology, history or sociology would have to be taught just as they are in the public schools, without any religious background or commentary whatever?"

When you ask the question, you receive three types of answers. Some earnest campaigners say they have never heard of the condition, any more than most Catholics have who have attended the rallies or read the campaign literature. Other workers give that small, sympathetic, you-must-have-been-born-yesterday smile that makes one understand that English literature, science and history would continue to be taught quite safely in the good old Catholic way, except when the state supervisor happened to drop in. Hard core proponents, in some states, explain that their bill, unlike some, does not expressly provide that religious views and values may not be mentioned in presenting the subject. Therefore, as long as the secular aspects of the subject are taught as fully as they are in the public schools, religious permeation would be entirely legal.

We can deal with the uninformed. We cannot deal with the dishonest. We can only wonder what constitutional expert advised the honest and zealous third group that when a secular subject is permeated with religious values in a private school it is still a secular subject in the sense forced by the courts upon the public schools. This is the only sense the word "secular" may constitutionally have when used in a statute which provides public moneys for schools. In the public schools "secular" means "secular," period. No Supreme Court will permit it to mean "secular plus" in private schools. Not until hell freezes over and prayer and Bible reading are again permitted in the public schools will this happen. The kind of sophistication that holds that any religion is better for our children than no religion and hence may be taught in the public schools is not yet present among a majority of Catholics, Jews, Protestants or Supreme Court justices. Unless public sentiment shifts to that point of view, significant public aid will not be declared legal for schools that remain religious in purpose and practice.

What is the right Catholic answer to this dilemma? Should we compromise by gradually secularizing our schools to gain public aid? Should we work for relaxation of the constitutional principle so that we may get the aid without the compromise but with the result that those of our children who attend public schools will be subjected to any religion?. Or shall we avoid both horns of the dilemma by financing our schools ourselves?

To the Catholic Community as a Whole

Before leaving the subject of public aid, it might be well to illustrate with an example or two the significance of the table in Appendix A and anticipate a question or two that the table itself does not answer.

In a television interview in January, 1969, Cardinal Cody said that the cost of educating the 325,000 students then in the Catholic schools in the Chicago archdiocese was $90,000,000 a year, whereas it would cost $225,000,000 to educate the same children in the public schools. This is a per pupil cost ratio of 2 to 5. At least half of the Chicago taxpayers are Catholic. It would be no advantage to Catholics there if the Catholic schools were to close. It would then cost them $112,500,000 to educate their children. Are the Cardinal and his pastors tired of persuading their people to contribute the $90,000,000? Have they decided to relax and let the taxgatherers collect the $112,500,000 from their people—or, for awhile, some part of the $90,000,000? Apparently so, for the cardinal gave his unqualified support to a bill sponsored in 1969 by the Citizens for Educational Freedom to provide public aid to the schools by direct payments to the schools under the purchased public service theory. Thus Illinois Catholics would fit under Columns IV or VI in the Appendix A table.

The bill sponsored by the Citizens for Educational Freedom in Wisconsin in 1969 and officially backed by the bishops of the state called for tuition reimbursements to parents under the child welfare theory. Wisconsin Catholics would find their situation shown in Columns III or V of the table.

In Milwaukee, incidentally, the ratio of per pupil costs is said to be 1 to 3. At least 35% of the Milwaukee taxpayers are Catholic. If the stated cost ratio is correct, every child who leaves a Catholic school in Milwaukee moves the cost of his education from the Catholic community on a voluntary contribution basis to the Catholic community on a compulsory tax basis. This relieves the Catholic school authorities of the burden of collecting voluntary contributions, but it is of no financial advantage to the Catholic community. The individual parent, of course, does not see the effect of moving his children to the public school. But why are not all Catholic parents insistently warned of the ultimate cost disadvantage when many parents transfer their children from Catholic to public schools? They might then persuade themselves and their Catholic friends to stay with the Catholic schools and work for their improvement.

In presenting the above examples, we do not claim that the cost figures given by any Catholic school authority today represent the precise cost of Catholic education. Such figures will be accurate only when a uniform system of cost accounting is required of all schools and the figures are subject to independent audit to be sure that the system is being consistently followed by all concerned. This does not imply dishonesty. Whatever cost figures are obtainable are honestly reported. Accurate figures are simply not obtainable because of the lack of modern cost accounting.

Furthermore, even if today's stated local cost ratios of 2 to 5 or 1 to 3 or 1 to 2, are reasonably correct, the ratios are bound to narrow considerably in the foreseeable future. Nevertheless, the ratio will never reach 1 to 1 and will probably stabilize at about 4 to 5. (The basis for this assertion is given in the explanatory notes of Appendix C.) If to the cost to Catholic taxpayers of closing our schools, we add the cost of mounting an adequate CCD program, we are sure to find that we would be financially better off in many dioceses (including all of the ten or twelve largest dioceses). And we would not be much worse off in the other dioceses if we gathered our forces and vigorously pursued the old goal of every Catholic child in a Catholic school. (See the example and the conclusions drawn from it in Appendix D.) Under all the circumstances, it would seem highly preferable if the bishops would present these facts to us and at least give us a chance to rise to the challenge of increasing our contributions, instead of trying to frighten the general public with the threat of higher taxes.

Another practical consideration or two: our grade schools are generally supported by parish contributions; our high schools are generally supported by tuition. Contributions are tax deductible; tuition payments are not. Aside from the desirability of all of our schools being tuition-free like the public schools so that the children of the poor can attend them without loss of dignity, the contribution method of financing all of our schools would automatically result in substantial public support through the operation of the federal income tax system. Under that system, the taxpayer's cost of a contribution is reduced by a percentage equal to the highest tax bracket he would reach without deducting the amount of the contribution from his otherwise taxable income. The amount of that tax saving is shifted to others. But, of course, to the extent that he and those making similar contributions are a proportion of the "others," they must make up the initial saving.

Appendix E shows that the total effect of this system would result in a net shifting to the non-Catholic public of 20% of the cost of supporting our schools wholly by contributions from the Catholic community. The calculations in Appendices A, B, C and D are based upon this positive effect of the federal income tax system.

Are the bishops and the school authorities unaware of this tax effect? Or are they afraid to rely upon voluntary contributions? Or is 20% public support believed to be insufficient? In any event, they suggest that we ask for $50 per grade school pupil per year and $100 per high school pupil per year from the state. This approximates one-fifth of present costs. That is why the comparisons in the Appendix A table are based upon a one-fifth level of state aid. The table shows the insignificant value at best (columns III and IV) and the negative value at worst (columns V and VI) of aid at that level to the Catholic community as a whole.

The sad fact is that columns V and VI more closely indicate the actual situation that would exist under the public aid proposals than columns III and IV. This is true because in order to qualify for the form of public aid represented by the child welfare theory the schools would be obliged to charge tuition in at least the amount of the grants. The high schools, of course, already subsist on tuition rather than contributions (except for occasional supplementary diocesan aid). To the extent that all of the schools move toward the tuition method of financing, the net Catholic cost picture will move toward columns V and VI. The moral is the same one that has been pointed out before and will be emphasized again: the best way to finance all of our schools is by contributions, rather than by tuition. We realize, indirectly and painlessly, nearly as much public aid by that means of financing as by the amounts of direct public aid now being proposed under the purchased public service theory, and more than that being proposed under the child welfare theory.

To the Individual Catholic

That is the picture for the Catholic community as a whole. Let us see what $50 of public aid would be worth to the individual Catholic.

Paid to a parent under the child welfare theory, it would probably, and definitely after the fourth annual payment per child, constitute taxable income to him. So it would be worth to him a maximum of $43, a minimum of $15. The $50 would come from the state having been raised by taxes. In Illinois and Wisconsin and many other of the most populous states where Catholics constitute 30% or more of the population, the parent would have paid (in advance, in the form of his share of various forms of state taxes) at least $15. So the $50 would be worth to him a maximum of $28 a year, a minimum of zero. No need to figure what taxes he would save by contributing the $50 to the school. Any school still living by contributions would be "obliged" to adopt a tuition schedule equalling or exceeding the $50 in order to be sure to extract the "aid" from the parent, even if it were not a provision of the law, as it is, that the tuition be paid by the parent first, in order to qualify for the grant.

Direct payments to the schools under the purchased public service theory would have greater net value. Only the Catholics' share of the taxes raised to pay it would reduce it (in Illinois and Wisconsin, for example, to about $35). But, of course, parents get their hands on none of the money under this plan. Neither do Catholics who do not have children in a Catholic school. Under both the child welfare and the purchased services schemes, these Catholics would have to pay their share of the taxes to finance the grants, with nothing coming back. They would be forced to pay what they should be persuaded to contribute voluntarily.

Some proponents of the child welfare type of aid appear to rely on the possibility that tuition reimbursements to parents will be classed as scholarships under federal income tax regulations, and hence exempt from tax. Parents expecting to rely upon the exemption would be well advised to consult a good tax attorney first. Even if the attorney should advise that the payments constitute scholarships, he would be obliged to add that, under the present law, scholarships are exempt for only thirty-six months of schooling (about four school years) per child. The exemption is lifetime, and any scholarship received by or in behalf of the child beyond the thirty-six months would be fully taxable. A parent who claimed the exemption of $50 for Dan and $50 for Dee for four years in the grades would have to pay full tax on the $100 received for each in high school. Furthermore, if Dan should receive a $500 college scholarship and Dee a $2,500 one, each would find that because their Dad took the $50 exemption in the grades they are disqualified from claiming exemption for any part of their college scholarships. A trap for the unwary indeed! Mention of this facet of the child welfare proposal is apparently verboten.

What is to be thought of the public aid proposal strategies? If we believe that public aid is both necessary and safe, we can at least see that the purchased public service theory is of considerably greater financial benefit. And in some states it stands a greater chance of being declared constitutional than the child welfare theory. We might even agree that any compromise of the principle of religious-secular integration should never extend beyond the very few subjects that are really not susceptible of such treatment.

But if the principle is established, public aid will lead eventually to the destruction of our schools as religious schools and in our greed, or alleged need for public assistance we will compromise religious permeation out of more and more subjects. For public aid will never be approved by the courts except on the "secular subject" condition. So we advocate persuading the Catholic community to use a Christian approach, rather than to induce the public to use a practical approach. If we accept public aid, our worst present problem, the closed, unreachable administration of our schools will be aggravated. At very least, that situation must be corrected in the best interests of both the Catholic and the general community before aid is sought or voted. To repeat, the writer views with dismay the failure of the public aid advocates to disclose to the Catholic community the slim to negative dollar advantage of the aid proposals. At times he is inclined to categorize the strategy to get public aid as one that was conceived with the cunning of an old-world peasant and guided through the legislative halls with the power plays of a Tammany Hall politician. In his calmer moments, he deplores it as a vote of non-confidence in the intelligence, good-will and generosity of the laity.

The Responsibilities of the Bishops

It may seem to some readers, especially to any bishop who may be reading this book, that an inordinate amount of space has been devoted to criticism of the bishops. Despite the high decibel level of some of the criticism, we hope they will regard it as constructive. Its purpose is twofold: first, to bring to the attention of the bishops some facts regarding the unrealistic and destructive course being pursued to keep the schools alive, and to suggest an alternate course in administration and financing which might be more difficult to follow but which is nevertheless practical and constructive. And, second, we want to encourage them to believe that the laity will support them if they will adopt the more difficult but more Christian approach.

At any rate, let me state emphatically that I am not directing any criticism at any bishop as a person. It is directed to the bishops ex officio as ordinaries of the people of God whom they have been ordained to serve as apostles in spiritual affairs and as trustees in temporal ones. My purpose is to persuade the bishops that Catholics will follow, if they will exercise leadership primarily by straight-forward teaching of authentic Christian spirituality; and secondarily, but as an essential condition to the success of the teaching mission, by being frank with the laity regarding the temporalities involved in that mission. The latter point is essential because the day is past when the oft-repeated hierarchical admonition, "Just have faith in us," will gain followers. Faith in the hierarchy will be the response today only of those in whom the hierarchy has first shown confidence—confidence in their faith, in their good will, in their fidelity and in their competence.

Quite obviously, the bishops as a whole have failed to show this confidence. Whether the criticism is justified in every respect must be left to the readers, including the bishops, to judge. But to the extent it is justified, it is a very serious matter.

Directors and officers of business corporations have been forced out of office, or have been required to pay damages, or have been penalized by government regulatory agencies for having failed to furnish their stockholders or prospective investors with sufficient information, or sufficiently accurate information to enable them to make intelligent decisions about the business. These directors and officers were said to have breached the duty of disclosure, a duty arising out of their trust or fiduciary relationship to their stockholders and the investing public. Some of the failures to disclose were not markedly different from the lack of candor with which the bishops have treated the administration and financing of the schools, not least their failure to present the total picture with respect to proposals for public aid. Courts have taken an unsympathetic view of the defense often put forward by directors or officers that they "did not know" certain significant facts about the business. The law charges corporate officials with such knowledge, that is, the law presumes that corporate officials know all important facts and conditions affecting the business, within the business or outside it, which they could have learned if they had been reasonably diligent.

It is sadly anomalous when it appears that the secular conscience expressed in statutes and court decisions is more sensitive than the religious conscience with respect to obligations of disclosure and truthfulness to properly interested persons concerning important temporal matters. Why should a religious conscience need a law to educate, to sensitize it? It seems to be a matter of paternalism corrupting confidence. Unwittingly, but nevertheless tragically, paternalism tends to corrupt the mutual confidence of its agents and its subjects alike.

Compassion for an executive of a business or any other institution who is inescapably overworked and plagued with problems only he can handle—the truly indispensable man—is one thing. But it is not uncharitable to suggest that an executive who overloads himself with administrative details and frets solo over decisions that could just as well be delegated to others to handle or to participate in may have chiefly himself to blame if he ends distraught, impatient, difficult and ultimately ineffective in service to his principals. In justice to the corporation or community he serves, he should learn to delegate or share responsibilities and authority. Above all, he should learn to keep the people he serves informed of all matters affecting their common interests. To sum up, he should display confidence in them.

Financing the Schools by the Catholic Community

If the forms of public aid now being sought in state legislatures would be a setting sun and not a new dawn in the future of Catholic education, what is the solution of the money problem? Because of the decline in school enrollments, the closing of some schools, the increasing need for lay teachers to replace religious and the rising cost of buildings, supplies and especially salaries, the question naturally arises whether the required money can be raised within the Catholic community itself.

Two important facts should be known about Catholic educational financing: present costs and ultimate costs. This includes not just bare costs, but the expense of financing our schools compared to costs of closing the schools and placing the children in the public schools, plus conducting an adequate CCD program. To put it another way, what is the present extra cost, and what is the ultimate extra cost of maintaining a system of Catholic schools? Both facts are important. We must know today's extra cost in order to realize that the financing burden is not any greater than it has ever been. And we must know the ultimate extra cost in order to see that with additional, but manageable, sacrifice it can be met.

Of the two, ultimate cost is probably the most important. It seems incontrovertible that the reason for the present crisis is not present expenses but the fear that school budgets are gradually becoming too large to support and that the wise thing to do is to prepare for the day when the schools will be forced to close. This is undoubtedly one of the reasons why enrollment in the elementary schools is declining so drastically. Many parents are deciding not to enroll their children in schools which they fear will close before their children have completed eighth or twelfth grade. This is not an unreasonable position if their fears are justified. But they are entitled to know the facts. Furthermore, good planning of any venture demands a realistic appraisal of the ultimate possibility of carrying it on.

Comparative Extra Cost from Generation to Generation

Appendices B, C, D and E should be studied carefully at this point in the discussion. Appendix C is the most important because it illustrates the ultimate extra cost of maintaining Catholic schools in communities having various percentages of Catholics in the total population and with various percentages of Catholic children in Catholic schools. Appendix D is an illustration of present extra costs in a particular community. Both appendices use the same method of calculating extra cost. Hence, either may be used to determine extra cost in any community whatever by simply substituting local population, school enrollment and per pupil cost figures.

Appendix B shows the relative extra cost from generation to generation. It takes the Catholic community as a national whole, and suggests a national financing system. It is also the source of the prediction that the extra cost of Catholic education may ultimately be 30% higher than at present.

Appendix E shows two things: where the real money is, and the correctness of the assumption, frequently emphasized in this book, that 20% is a realistic figure to use as the amount of potential savings by financing with contributions. We should not forget that additional saving would be realized in states with personal income tax systems modelled after the federal one.

The explanatory notes accompanying the Appendix C tables repeat several basic concepts presented in the main text that cannot be emphasized too much. In the first place, the only realistic basis for determining whether or not the maintenance of our schools is possible is to compare their cost with the cost to us of closing the schools and sending our children to the public schools. What counts is not the comparative cost to us as against the cost to our non-Catholic neighbors. All that such comparisons lead to is demoralizing self-pity about unjust financial burdens. They make us feel sorry for ourselves and angry at our neighbors. That gets us nowhere. It clouds with emotion our reasoning about the fundamental decision we must make: despite the inevitable extra burden we bear as compared with our non-Catholic neighbors, is the maintenance of our separate schools worth the sacrifice?

In the second place, the only true basis for determining the actual extra cost is to take into account our position as taxpayers. All we hear about taxes in connection with the schools is that we are subjected to double taxation. The Appendix C and D tables disclose that we are never doubly taxed. "Double taxation" is another emotional term used in arguments for public aid and has no literal truth in it. What needs understanding and emphasis are the positive aspects of the tax system. What counts is the net extra cost to us of maintaining our schools compared to closing them and placing our children in the public schools after taking all taxes into account. The tables show this real net extra cost. But the tables reflect a third basic concept: our schools should be financed by contributions rather than by tuition to maximize the positive aspects of the tax system.

From the Appendix C and D tables it is possible for anyone to determine what the real net extra cost is in his community today, and what it is likely to be ultimately. All he needs to know to determine today's situation is the percentage of Catholics in the total population in his community, the percentage of Catholic children in the Catholic schools and the Catholic school-public school per pupil costs and cost ratios. All he needs to do to determine the future situation is to find out from his local newspaper or Chamber of Commerce what the Catholic to general population trends are, assume that any particular goal for getting Catholic children into Catholic schools has been reached, and expect the worst for per pupil cost ratios. The Appendix C tables estimate that the worst ratio will be 1 to 1¼. It is unlikely that future experience will prove that any miscalculations or faulty assumptions in the tables are of make-or-break consequence.

So, to determine the "extra cost" in any community today use the actual percentage of Catholics to the total population instead of the percentages used in the tables, the actual per pupil costs and cost ratios instead of the figures used in the tables and the actual percentage of Catholic children in the Catholic schools. Adjustments in the federal tax rates and percentages are unnecessary because these are the actual current national figures. So all you have to do is to carry through the arithmetic after ascertaining the local figures just mentioned. But if you are in a state which has a graduated income tax system like the federal one, include the additional tax saving by using the state tax rate equivalent to the federal 25% rate (that is, the rate applicable to a husband and wife joint return on the amount of their taxable income that exceeds $12,000), and adjust it in accordance with the Catholic population ratio in the state.

Appendix D is as an illustration of what such bridge-table-plus-pad-and-pencil research would show. It is an example based upon present day costs of education in a Wisconsin community in which Catholics constitute 30% of the population. Wisconsin has a graduated income tax system similar to the federal system, so it is characteristic of many other states in which Catholics constitute a significant percentage of the population. Get your Catholic neighbors and your pastor to play this parlor game with you, using the figures that apply in your community. It might help turn their discouragement about the support of their parish school into hope.

Just one caution: this do-it-yourself research will disclose what the "extra cost" is if the schools are supported by contributions instead of by tuition. To the extent that tuition is the actual practice and is likely to remain so, the formula used in the tables will have to be adjusted by modifying or omitting the tax savings calculations. Doing so will clearly demonstrate the advantage of financing completely by contributions.

Further illustrations would show that increases in percentages of Catholics and increases in the per pupil cost differential in favor of Catholic schools lowers the extra cost to Catholics so that it almost reaches zero. In communities with a Catholic population of 60% and a per pupil cost differential of 1 to 1½, the cost of the two choices (all the Catholic children in Catholic schools vs. all of them in public schools) almost balances. The same is true with a Catholic population of 45% and a cost differential of 1 to 2, or with a Catholic population of 77% and a cost differential of 1 to 1¼. In such situations, if Catholics close their schools they will have to pay as much as taxpayers to support the public school system as they now pay as Catholics and as taxpayers to support both systems. Pushing claims of justice to the point of threatening to close the Catholic schools in such situations or anything close to them does not make sense.

It is difficult to understand how under present conditions the Catholic school authorities in any city which is 30% or more Catholic should for a moment consider permanently abandoning any part of their primary or secondary school system. Surely money cannot be their problem. At least it should not be if they explained the economic facts of life to the people. Are they and their people whimperers? Has the spirit of our forefathers been lost somehow in our climb up the social and economic ladder to affluence? Are we no longer willing to pay the same price our forefathers did for the premium quality education we have always believed Catholic education uniquely to be?

Meeting Tomorrow's Extra Cost

So much for the possibilities of the present. What about the future? Can we sustain the schools through the period of mounting costs until ultimately the extra cost reaches 30% more than at present?

This is a challenge, indeed. In the first place, to be willing to pay such a premium we must realize that Catholic education is truly a premium education. The major part of this book has been devoted to the things that must be done to ensure that quality of Catholic education. We now must tackle the final question. Does the Catholic community have the money? How can we collect it, administer it economically and distribute it effectively?

We have the money. But new methods of obtaining money must be devised, and new methods of conserving and distributing it must be developed.

Too many research directors are preoccupied with what past contributions to Catholic educational causes have been. From that history they have determined priorities among future educational programs. This is a predictably self-defeating approach to mounting the kind of comprehensive educational effort described in this book. Priorities among educational programs should be based upon mission needs, not upon money needs, and certainly not upon historical money collection figures. The latter lead to complacency with past efforts and discouragement about increasing them. Research should be devoted to what money we need to finance the programs we know we should have now and in the foreseeable future. Then we should decide how that amount of money can be obtained.

The Catholic community as a whole should supply the money for Catholic education. To get the Catholic community to do anything as a community will be quite a task, but we are only asking that Catholics begin to act like Christians, that is, like authentic Catholics. Suggestions regarding this task were treated in the chapter on structures. For the moment let us assume that substantial advances in that direction will be made.

The Catholic community of today is no longer a group of immigrants at the bottom of the economic ladder. Our grandfathers and great-grandfathers were. Yet they and their sons, who were better off than they were but still below us on the economic scale, built and maintained churches and schools at a higher rate in proportion to their resources than we. Whether it is literally true that St. Patrick's Cathedral was built with the nickels and dimes of the Irish servant maids of New York, it is undoubtedly true that the

Irish, the Germans, the Italians, the Poles and all of the others who built the churches and schools we still enjoy today were desperately poor.

On the other hand, we constitute about one-fourth of the population of these United States, and as a group we are as well off as any comparable cross section of people in the country. Our "economic profile," as the expression goes, is at least as favorable as that of the country as a whole. It is probably more favorable because the country as a whole contains a higher percentage of the poor and the destitute than does the Catholic population. We have become a Church of the middle classes. (Let no reader be disturbed at the use of the term, "middle class." It is intended to express an economic fact, not a moral judgment.)

A study of Appendix B will show basic implications of the change in our situation in the relative extra cost from generation to generation to finance Catholic schools. It shows that the extra cost to us of supporting the schools is only slightly higher than it was for our forefathers. It shows, furthermore, that even if our school costs should at some future date approach those of the public schools (which is probable, though not yet foreseeable), the extra cost to the Catholic community of supporting its own schools alongside the public schools would be only about 30% more, relatively, than the present extra cost of doing so.

Some one at this point may say to himself: "So we are better off than our parents and grandparents. But what with taxes and inflation we are still poor. Why, just yesterday it was announced that the cost-of-living index went up another two-tenths of a percent last month. How can we expect to send our children to college, the way tuition is skyrocketing?"

It might be difficult to persuade many of our Catholic neighbors, who, like everyone else, are unconsciously floating on the tide of rising expectations and consciously trying to keep up with their neighbors, that compared with their grandfathers they are staggeringly, swaggeringly rich. A man hears that his grandfather paid five cents for a loaf of bread for which he now pays thirty cents. He forgets that his grandfather worked half an hour at ten cents an hour for that loaf. He worked less than five minutes at four dollars an hour for it. He wonders whether he can get the mortgage on his house paid in time to send his kids to college. He forgets that his grandfather could not dream of sending his kids to college even if the college was located in the same town. The boys were lucky if they were able to finish high school before they had to go to work to assist the family.

Just as the cost of a loaf of bread of a given size and quality has actually decreased in terms of any absolute standard of measurement such as the number of hours of work required to purchase such a loaf, so also the cost of any particular package of education, whether in a grade school, a high school, or a college has decreased in terms of the relative ability of the Catholic parent to pay for it. If the cost of an education has increased relatively, it is only because the quality of the educational package has been improved.

The National Industrial Conference Board is a nonprofit research organization supported by businessmen to tell them facts of life, not dreams or fantasies. Business men use its information to guide their planning and to supplement their own market research with broader and deeper facts about the economy as a whole. The Conference Board's research figures are accurate, and its forecasts seldom miss by more than a hair.

On the point we are discussing, namely, the effect of taxes and inflation on real income, the Conference Board in mid 1969 issued a report illustrated with a series of charts titled "The Consumer of the Seventies." The report's most significant disclosures concerning our feeling of being "poor," are that since the end of World War II in 1945, gross national product and disposable personal income increased at a rate of a little more than 4% a year, while population increased less than 1.5% a year. Roughly translated, this means that our standard of living, the things we could buy with the hours of labor we expended, increased an average of more than 2.5% a year since 1945. The report predicts that those growth rates will continue throughout the 1970's, probably at somewhat accelerated rates, just as other studies have shown that the 4% rates prevailing in the 1960's were preceded by 3% rates before World War II and 2% rates still earlier in the history of our economy. Our standard of living and our real incomes have skyrocketed and will continue to do so.

The Prudential Insurance Company issues an economic forecast each year. Its forecast of November, 1969, presented figures on the growth of the gross national product and disposable personal incomes that matched the figures given by the Conference Board. It also presented the effect of taxes and inflation on real income. Noting the increasingly adverse effects of both of these factors since 1965, when a major step-up in the Vietnam War took place, it nevertheless predicted that the present high level of both will taper off in 1970 and 1971. It also showed that in the period 1960 to 1970, gross family incomes grew 75%. And even after taking into account taxes and inflation, real family incomes grew 30%—a cool 3% a year. In the 1970's gross family income will again increase 75 or 80%, and real family income, again after taking taxes and inflation into account, will rise 40%—a cool 4% a year! The country's largest banks, Chase Manhattan, National City and Morgan Guaranty have published the same predictions.

This is why, despite increased costs, our generation is actually able to support our schools more easily than our forefathers did. That is why future generations will be able to support the schools at least as easily as we can.

By retaining our schools we are not passing an unsupportable burden on to our children. The possible 30% increase in extra cost will be offset within ten years, at the rate of at least 3% a year. The rate of increase in extra cost will not always match the rate of increase in real income, and in those periods when the former gets ahead of the latter we may tend to panic as we have in the recent year or two of notable inflation. But the two will average out to a match within the ten-year period. Even an economic recession would delay the complete offset effect only a year or two, and a full-blown depression would delay it only four or five years. If we keep our faith in our country and its progressive economy as well as in our schools, the adjustment to the higher level of extra cost should be fairly painless.

This factual picture should make us wonder if we do not deserve to be called the whimpering generation.

The Conference Board's predictions as to the directions in which money will be spent in the 1970's are also most interesting. Continuing already existing spending habits, we will spend 3% more for alcohol and tobacco, 3.5% more for food, 5% more for shelter, 6% more for higher education, 6.5% more for automobiles and 8% more for radio, TV and records. These are the marks of a truly affluent society. We Catholics share this affluence to the same degree as the rest of the population. The Catholic community is affluent and is destined to become wealthier. We should be ashamed to whimper.

This money picture clearly gives us no cause for defeatism. It challenges only our sense of value. What shall we opt for if our family budget pinches—bigger and better houses, cars, TV sets, or more and better programs of Catholic education? The question is as simple as that if the family budget really pinches.

The Conference Board presents the national picture which is not an irrelevant one in terms of the Catholic community as a whole. But it is possible to get the same kinds of facts about local areas, including each of the cities of the country. Anyone interested in learning how affluent his local community is and just where the money is there, can find out with assurance of only inconsequential error by studying the annual publication of *Sales Management: Magazine of Marketing* called *Survey of Buying Power.** A copy can probably be found in the reference room of the public library. If not, it can be obtained from the publisher. Its findings and conclusions are also in extensive tables and charts compiled by the local newspaper and printed in one of the year-end or first of the year issues, along with many other types of information relevant to our subject, such as population, denominational memberships, school enrollments (private as well as public), number of families, number of wage earners, average earnings and the like.

It is not necessary for the 250 or so dioceses in the country to spend $50,000 each for a research program to dig up parish contribution records for the last ten years and then extrapolate them to see whether the diocese can support its schools. Everyone knows that contributions have been trending downward, and a fifteen-year-old boy could predict that the extrapolation line would run off the bottom of the page. The figures the Catholic population

* 630 Third Ave., New York, N.Y. 10017.

needs to know, and to know that everyone else knows, including the bishops and the school authorities, is what amount could the Catholic population contribute with relative comfort if they had a cause they considered worthy. By studying the readily obtainable figures described above, half a dozen ordinary laymen in each diocese could ascertain all that needs to be known about how much money is practically available from whom for Catholic education in their diocese and each significant area within it.

Such a study would show, for instance, that freely disposable, after-tax income (what *Sales Management* calls "Effective Income") was distributed in 1968 approximately as follows. (Only a few states of particular interest to Catholics are shown here. Arkansas and Mississippi are shown because they are the poorest of the states.)

	Average EI per Household	Households w/less than $8,000 EI	EI in their hands	Households w/$8,000 or more EI	EI in their hands
U.S. as a whole	$ 9512	57%	28%	43%	72%
New York	10662	52%	24%	48%	76%
Pennsylvania	9616	56%	29%	44%	71%
Massachusetts	10545	52%	27%	48%	73%
Connecticut	11763	45%	21%	55%	79%
New Jersey	10902	49%	24%	51%	76%
Ohio	9759	54%	27%	46%	73%
Illinois	11489	44%	18%	56%	82%
Wisconsin	10045	51%	25%	49%	75%
Missouri	8679	63%	42%	37%	58%
California	10180	53%	24%	47%	76%
Mississippi	6848	74%	41%	26%	59%
Arkansas	6707	75%	44%	25%	56%

The broken down figures in every state show that rural areas bring down the average incomes. The wealth is largely concentrated in the cities and the so-called metropolitan areas. This explains in large part, if not completely, why largely urban states like New York and Connecticut have average incomes so much higher than largely rural states like Mississippi and Arkansas. City figures are invariably more favorable than their state's figures.

Does all of this suggest anything? Certainly. The real money is in the hands of from one-third to one-half of the population, concentrated in the metropolitan areas, and they receive from two-thirds to three-fourths of the freely disposable, after-tax income of the population. Appendix E contains federal income tax figures which illustrate the same point.

It should be abundantly clear that the Catholic community has

Eliminating Inequities within the Catholic Community

the money to support a complete school system now and in the future without public aid. Two points mentioned earlier remain: how to gather the money and how to conserve and distribute it. Specific suggestions on both points were made in the discussion of centralization in the chapter on structure. A few general remarks, however, will be added here.

We have emphasized contributions rather than tuition as the source of funds for the schools. This recommendation is based upon more than the practical tax-saving effect of that method, important as that consideration is. The contribution method leads to more specifically Christian results—the formation of community and the achievement of justice within that community. It must seem odd to outsiders that while we struggle for justice from the civic community we seem to neglect the requirements of justice within the Catholic community.

It is doubtful that at any time more than half of the members of the Catholic community have contributed significantly to the support of the schools. Not only do most Catholics in those parishes without schools contribute nothing, but even in parishes with schools it is usually the parents who have children in the schools who bear the greater part of the financial burden as long as their children are in the schools. Contributions from all parishioners all their earning lives in accordance with their ability is precisely in line with the long-enforced obligation of every citizen to pay taxes for support of the tuition-free public schools whether he has children in them or not. Catholic school financing, like public school financing, should be a common obligation freely and gladly accepted, and the schools should be tuition-free.

Another point relates to justice within the Catholic community. It is apparent that some parishes are able to support an adequate grade school; some are not. Without changing the traditional system of placing basic responsibility on the parish for providing a school, the desirability of wealthier parishes assisting poorer ones either directly or through diocesan fund drives is indicated. If we do not somehow arrange for tuition-free grade schools in poorer parishes, lower income groups will be alienated from the Church within a generation. Blaming our failure on the parish school setup (as the neighborhood school setup is blamed for inequalities in the public school system) would make the alienation quicker and more complete.

A similar problem of unequal ability exists with respect to the financing of high schools. This suggests that the high schools be financed by tuition at a level to cover costs, that this tuition be assessed to the parishes for their children who attend the school, and that the normal diocesan fund drive for charitable and other needs be enlarged to include deficits in collections from poorer parishes. The parishes would not charge the tuition to the parents of the children. They would collect the amount of their assessment by contributions from the whole parish.

Some dioceses are able on this two-level financing basis to finance all their school needs; some are not. This suggests the desirability of the wealthier dioceses assisting the poorer ones, either directly or through a national Catholic system of school aids based on need, similar to the proposed comprehensive federal aid system for public schools. (Note that the suggestion is national aid, not national administration.)

More Ways To Save Time and Money

As to the conservation and efficient distribution of funds, the benefits of centralization at a diocesan or intradiocesan area level are so manifest that only a brief word will be put down here. Significant savings could be achieved by group self-insurance or blanket insurance, central architectural services, central furnishing of educational specialists and TV educational programs, central buying of textbooks, educational aids, fuel and supplies and central planning and control of building programs. Additional significant savings could be realized by a rigorous policy of competitive bidding and the placement of contracts and purchase orders to the lowest responsive and responsible bidder. In addition to the usual conditions concerning technical and financial qualifications, "responsible bidder" would mean nondiscrimination in employment.

Central administration of the gathering and distribution of funds is a recognition of the principle that school financing is the responsibility of the entire Catholic community. In practice it means diocesan-level collections for the schools to be distributed to parishes which need supplementary aid so that equal educational facilities, tuition-free, may be provided to all children. This is the most obvious and immediate benefit.

Corporations are potential sources of contributions to support schools. Such contributions are deductible for federal income tax purposes to the same extent as are state and local tax payments. However, businessmen need to be shown that dollars contributed to particular private schools pay for as good education of future citizens as the same amount of dollars paid as taxes for support of the public schools, and that there is a single official place to which contributions for that purpose can be sent with assurance that they will be effectively used to provide such education. As a clincher, we must show businessmen that their contributions for which they get the same income tax deduction as they get for state and local taxes provide the desired quality of education to *more* children than their tax dollars and, therefore their donations actually reduce their potential total outlay for education.

Private colleges have found from experience the importance of having a single receipt and distribution center for contributions from corporations. Corporations and charitable foundations find it impossible to determine the worthiness of requests of the same type from a multitude of sources—such as 50 or 100 or 200 individual Catholic grade and high schools. So they do not contribute to any of them. But if a central diocesan office existed and the business community learned that contributions sent to it would be distributed equitably and efficiently to the Catholic schools in the community, many such contributions might be forthcoming. Private colleges have learned the practical value of establishing central offices to which contributions may be sent. Contributions to the colleges from business sources by this method are steadily increasing. In some states, Chambers of Commerce and associations of manufacturers publicize and advocate such giving by their members.

In doing so, the business associations stress the point that the education given is not only as good as that given by the tax-supported institutions but that more students per dollar receive it. It should not be impossible to persuade a practical businessman in a given community to overcome possible feelings of exclusive loyalty to the public school system by demonstrating that $1,000 contributed to the Catholic schools in his community will go two or three times as far as $1,000 paid in taxes for the public schools. In a word, it is to his substantial financial advantage to help support the Catholic schools in order to prevent the portion of his tax dollar that goes for public school education (about 50% in older communities, up to 75% in newer ones) from doubling or trebling if the Catholic schools are forced to phase out.

There may be still another desirable effect of trying to achieve a community approach to financing education. Working on this tangible cause might help us work as a community on all of the other problems and tasks that involve, or ought to involve, the people of God. One particular application of this idea involves both the matter of community and the matter of money. Some Catholics complain that parishes devote too much effort and money to the "child-centered preoccupation called the parish school." They seem to suggest that if we directed our activities toward the Catholic education of adults and our money toward other causes, never clearly specified, we would all be better Christians for it.

A large portion of this book has been devoted to the proposition that if our sights are where they ought to be, on the future of the Church, the education of children has a higher priority and greater worth as a community effort than the education of adults. Furthermore, some acute observers say that a parish school provides the only community effort that exists in most parishes. These observers conclude that without the school, the parish would have little

activity as a community, and the charge that the parish is dysfunctional and passé might become justified. These observers suggest
that the situation would improve if the parish broadened its vision
and activities from school to education and moved seriously toward
the Catholic education of adults and children who are in the public
schools. But they point out that they have at least the school to
start with.

We heartily agree with this observation, and we also believe in
geographically defined parishes. If our goal is community formation,
the fractioning of parishioners into right little, tight little groups of
like-minded friends would prove dysfunctional. Parishes, like family
farms, may have an optimal size in a given place. Much better, for
instance, that a big city parish of 2,000 families be divided into two or
three parishes of more or less equal size, and that the 500 Catholic
families in a town of 6,000 people merge their two ethnic parishes.
However this may be, it seems more Christian for a parish to make a
Christian community out of the diverse people within its geographical limits, and from that center make a better civic community out
of its area.

Let us, however, quit this digression and return to the question of
what other purposes a parish might find for the money it would save
if it closed its school. Experience shows that money is contributed to
meet almost any need that is understood, seldom more, sometimes
less. Parish contributions usually match the parish budget. Usually
only unpopular or poorly publicized causes fail. At the same time,
no one contributes what he believes is more than his fair share toward
the parish budget. For instance, when the parish debt has been paid,
contributions drop to the operation expense level. If a parishioner has
greater resources and a generous heart, he contributes to his favorite
mission or charity.

What cause would a parish substitute for its school? A CCD program? It would certainly have a CCD program, but not as a substitute for the school. A CCD program for all the children would cost
nearly as much money; it would be just as child-centered, and for
the reasons set forth in the first part of this book, it would be inferior
to the school as a means for providing the children an integrated
Catholic education. Adult education courses? Surely, but they would

require comparatively little money. Social action programs, foreign missions? That would be the day! Revenues would not be switched from the school to other causes. They would simply not be contributed. Ironically, the very ability to contribute to other programs would be reduced by higher taxes imposed upon the members of the Catholic community as a result of the closing of the school and placing the children in the more expensive public school.

The Response Ability of the Individual Catholic

One final point about money for Catholic education. It moves the discussion from the community at large, the local community and the possibility of help from others right down to the individual Catholic. This means the discussion involves not only my neighbor; it also involves me.

The table in Appendix F shows what the average taxpayer claimed in his 1966 Federal income tax return as deductions for interest, taxes, medical expense, miscellaneous other deductible items and charitable and religious contributions. The table is damning proof of a materialistic society. From Appendix E we see that 99.5% of taxpayers are in income brackets under $50,000. Appendix F shows that for these taxpayers, contributions run about half of interest payments as a percentage of income. It is apparent where the heart is. For interest is paid by the average taxpayer on a house mortgage and on balances due for an automobile, a TV set and other luxuries in the United States. It is particularly revealing that the poorest taxpayers among most taxpayers contributed to religious and charitable causes a larger proportion of their income than the wealthier ones did. As interest and tax payments go down as a proportion of income, contributions presumably could go up. Instead, they went down, too. Even the average taxpayer among the 0.5% of the most wealthy missed tithing by a country mile. It appears that for most of us, the more we get, the more we want—for ourselves.

The Internal Revenue Service publishes detailed figures every other year. The 1966 figures are the most recent ones available in mid 1970. They are practically identical with those disclosed by studies of the previous few years, so it is unlikely that there have been startling changes for the better in the last year or two with respect to our generosity toward good causes.

This is the picture of what Mr. Average Taxpayer and probably Mr. Average Catholic does with his money. Anyone of us can readily determine whether he did better or worse than Mr. Average Taxpayer. He can also study his own budget and decide whether it would not be fairly painless to give another $5, $10 or $15 a month, a rate of 4% or 5% of his after-tax income to support Catholic schools, including a fairly generous donation to his local community fund. Most of us could manage to do that without hurting our ability to provide decently for our family. If enough of us did it and put the amount of our intended contributions into the monthly budget as firmly as we do our scheduled payments for the car, the TV or the dishwasher, the financial support of an excellent Catholic educational system would be assured.

If any research is justified with respect to financing Catholic education, it is to obtain honest answers to the questions, "Who are contributing to the Church today? Are the contributors the old, the young, the well-to-do, the poor, the liberals, the conservatives? How does their present performance compare with their previous performance? And why?" While Appendix E shows where the real money is, and Appendix F shows that the average well-to-do taxpayer is comparatively less generous than the poorer one, the tables mask the performance of the average Catholic.

This point of information may be crucial to win support of the desired scope and quality for Catholic education. If it is true, as suggested earlier, that generosity to a cause is the best indication of belief in it, the knowledge of who is giving what to the Church would tell the bishops which people need to be resold on Catholic education and which people need to be recommitted to the faith itself. Meanwhile, until the opinion research experts figure out how to elicit honest answers to the foregoing questions, the bishops will have to use a spreadshot approach to all of us for contributions.

Recommitment to Christian Principles and Priorities

We will briefly recap the suggestions in this chapter. The relative extra cost of maintaining our present Catholic educational programs, which have been concentrated on the schools, will not increase. The only alternative to continuing to maintain the schools is to phase them out and join the public school system. But that would require us as taxpayers to pay the even higher costs there for the secular education of our children, and we would also have to pay for a parallel system almost as expensive to give children a religious education via CCD. In the long run, it would not cost much more to educate most of our children in our own schools than it would to educate some of them there and furnish a really adequate CCD religious education to the others, or to close the schools and rely upon CCD education of all our children.

Let us not be whimperers. Let us knuckle down to prove that ours is the most effective and economical educational system in the world. For our road to outside aid, whether from the government or from business, must pass through administrative efficiency and educational excellence. The sooner we modernize these areas, the sooner we will have a product in which the general public might be disposed to invest.

In capturing the support of the general public and responsible legislators, the convincing argument will not be fairness, justice, and the threat of higher taxes. It will be the demonstration of an equal or better education per tax dollar like Charles E. Wilson's "Bigger Bang for a Buck" argument for governmental efficiency during World War II. If we establish the kind of schools and systems of schools which this book describes and which the Catholic community itself comes to agree is deserved by it and worthy of it, it is quite possible that the general public may some day be glad to join us in solving the constitutional problem in such a way that we can preserve our schools without compromising their purpose as religious schools.

Meanwhile, let us be glad to pay the relatively small premium required to give our children quality education. And let us not dream away the days with visions of early, easily gained public aid. Let us look beyond the challenge and excitement of racking up one debating point after another in a campaign to win public aid. Let us first decide how or whether public aid could be accepted without destroying the purpose of our schools. Public aid should not be regarded as a mountain to be climbed just because it is there, or a moon to be reached for prestige and, hopefully, for more tangible benefits. In both those ventures, there are serious questions of priorities involved, if not serious possibilities of useless or disastrous results.

Let us prove to ourselves and to our neighbors that Catholic education is indeed the state's good servant in forming citizens of the highest character and competence, although it is, first of all, God's servant in forming saints. Our prior stress on forming saints is not in derogation of forming good citizens. It is its best practical guarantor. Let us prove that the citizen formed in our schools is interested, not just in himself or in his brethren in the Catholic community, but also in the well-being of his neighbors in the larger community. Let them say not just, "See those Christians, how they love one another," but, "See those Christians, how they love everyone."

There is a risk in this. Men sometimes hate those who show they love them. But this is the God-mandated Christian gamble.

Appendix A

After-Tax Cost to Catholics of Possible Methods of Financing Schools

	I By Tuition Only	II By Contributions Only
Gross Cost of Schools per $1,000	$1,000	$1,000
Catholics' Net Tax Deductions	None	200[1]
Net Catholic Payments	1,000	800
Net Non-Catholic Payments	None	200

III
By Contributions plus State-Reimbursed Tuition under Child Welfare Theory

Contributions	Reimbursed Tuition	
$800 plus	$200[2] =	$1,000
160 less	$\begin{cases} 60[3] \\ 50[4] \end{cases} =$	50
640 plus	110 =	750 (93.5%)[5]
160 plus	90 =	250 (125%)[5]

IV
By Contributions plus State Payments to Schools under Purchased Services Theory

Contributions	Grant	
$800 plus	$200[2] =	$1,000
160 less	60[3] =	100
640 plus	60 =	700 (87.5%)[5]
160 plus	140 =	300 (150%)[5]

V
By Unreimbursed Tuition plus State-Reimbursed Tuition under Child Welfare Theory

Tuition	Reimbursed Tuition	
$800 plus	$200[2] =	$1,000
None less	$\begin{cases} 60[3] \\ 50[4] \end{cases} =$	−110
800 plus	110 =	910 (114%)[5]
None plus	90 =	90 (45%)[5]

VI
By Unreimbursed Tuition plus State Payments to Schools under Purchased Services Theory

Tuition	Grant	
$800 plus	$200[2] =	$1,000
None less	60[3] =	−60
800 plus	60 =	860 (107.5%)[5]
None plus	140 =	140 (70%)[5]

Explanatory Notes

1. Federal personal income tax deductions, net. Assumes a 20% net saving. For explanation of this assumption, see Appendix E.
2. State payments under current proposals would equal about ⅕ of present annual per pupil costs in Catholic schools.
3. Various state taxes to finance the school aids. Assumes Catholics constitute 30% of population and hence of taxpayers of the state.
4. Federal personal income taxes at an average tax rate of 25%. In states having a graduated personal income tax system like the federal one, this "take-back" would be even higher. No "netting" is involved in this calculation.
5. As compared with Method II.

Appendix B

Comparative Extra Cost of Maintaining Catholic Schools
from Generation to Generation

The basis of the comparison is the cost to educate children in Catholic grade and high schools or to close Catholic schools and pay taxes to educate the same children in public schools.

At Present

Assumptions:
1. Catholics constitute 24% of the population and as a group enjoy the same characteristics of family size and income as the rest of the population (and hence pay taxes in proportion to their numbers);
2. Catholic schools are financed by contributions (not tuition) which qualify as federal income tax deductions at a net saving of 20% (for explanation of this assumption, see Appendix E);
3. Per pupil cost in public schools is 200% that in Catholic schools.

	In Catholic Schools	In Public Schools
Gross Cost	$1,000,000,000	$2,000,000,000
Catholics' Share	1,000,000,000	480,000,000 (24%)
Tax Savings (20%)	200,000,000	96,000,000
Net Catholic Share	800,000,000	384,000,000
Extra Cost to Catholics	416,000,000	

A Generation or So Ago

Assumptions:
1. Catholics constituted 20% of population and as a group enjoyed the same family size and income as the rest of the population (actually they were at a lower economic level);
2. Per pupil cost in public schools was 300% that in Catholic schools.

194

	In Catholic Schools	In Public Schools
Gross Cost	$1,000,000,000	$3,000,000,000
Catholics' Share	1,000,000,000	600,000,000 (20%)
Tax Savings	No income tax in effect	
Net Catholic Share	1,000,000,000	600,000,000
Extra Cost to Catholics	400,000,000	

A Generation or So Hence

Assumptions: 1. Catholics will constitute 26% of population and as a group will enjoy the same family size and income as the rest of the population;
2. Same assumption about Federal income tax effects as in the "At Present" example;
3. Per pupil cost in public schools will be 125% that in Catholic schools.

	In Catholic Schools	In Public Schools
Gross Cost	$1,000,000,000	$1,250,000,000
Catholics' Share	1,000,000,000	325,000,000 (26%)
Tax Savings (20%)	200,000,000	65,000,000
Net Catholic Share	800,000,000	260,000,000
Extra Cost to Catholics	540,000,000	

Explanatory Note

One billion dollars is used as the base to illustrate relative, not actual cost. Obviously $1,000,000,000 would cover the actual cost of educating more or fewer children from generation to generation. It is not absolute extra dollar cost but relative extra dollar cost that is important in making the decision whether it may be necessary to phase out our schools and send our children to the public schools.

The table shows that under the contribution method of financing and consequent tax savings, extra dollar cost is presently about 4% higher than it was a generation or so ago. In a generation or so in the future, at the highest probable point of cost as compared with the public schools, extra dollar cost via the contribution method of financing will become about 30% higher than it is today.

The table takes into account only three factors: percentage of Catholics to total population, Catholic vs. public school per pupil cost ratios and the operation of the federal personal income tax system. Additional potential savings from operation of state income tax systems are practically impossible to calculate on the total national basis represented in the table. More importantly, the factor of the increase in real income from generation to generation is not taken into account in the table. In other words, the relative extra dollar cost from generation to generation is shown, but the relative ability to pay that extra dollar cost is not shown. The latter factor is treated in the main text of the book. There it is shown that bearing the extra dollar cost is easier now than earlier, and that it is destined to become even easier.

Appendix C

Extra Burden and Extra Cost of Maintaining Catholic
Schools at Highest Probable Cost

Table 1—All of the Catholic Children in Catholic Schools

	Catholic School System	Public School System	Totals of Both Systems	Single System, Public Only
Population 20% Catholic				
Gross Cost	$1,000,000 (n children)	$5,000,000 (4n children)	$6,000,000 (5n children)	$6,250,000 (5n children)
Catholics' Share (20%)	1,000,000 (100%)	1,000,000 (20%)	2,000,000	1,250,000 (20%)
Tax Savings (20%)	200,000	200,000	400,000	250,000
Net Catholic Share	800,000	800,000	1,600,000	1,000,000
Share of Others	None	4,000,000 (80%)	4,000,000	5,000,000 (80%)
Tax Savings (6%)	None	240,000	240,000	300,000
Net Share of Others	None	3,760,000	3,760,000	4,700,000
Total Catholic Share	800,000	1,040,000	1,840,000	1,300,000
Total Share of Others	200,000	3,960,000	4,160,000	4,950,000
			1,200,000 (Prop. Cath. share—20%)	
			640,000 (Extra burden—53.3%)	540,000 (Extra Cost—41.5%)
Population 40% Catholic				
Gross Cost	$2,000,000 (2n children)	$3,750,000 (3n children)	$5,750,000 (5n children)	$6,250,000 (5n children)
Catholic Share	2,000,000 (100%)	1,500,000 (40%)	3,500,000	2,500,000 (40%)
Tax Savings (20%)	400,000	300,000	700,000	500,000
Net Catholic Share	1,600,000	1,200,000	2,800,000	2,000,000
Share of Others	None	2,250,000 (60%)	2,250,000	3,750,000 (60%)
Tax Savings (6%)	None	135,000	135,000	225,000

196

Net Share of Others	None	2,115,000	2,115,000	
Total Catholic Share	1,600,000	1,335,000	2,935,000	2,225,000
Total Share of Others	400,000	2,415,000	2,815,000	4,025,000
			2,300,000 (Prop. Cath. share—40%)	
			635,000 (Extra burden—27.6%)	710,000 (Extra Cost—31.9%)

Population 60% Catholic

Gross Cost	$3,000,000 (3n children)	$2,500,000 (2n children)	$5,500,000 (5n children)	$6,250,000 (5n children)
Catholic Share	3,000,000 (100%)	1,500,000 (60%)	4,500,000	3,750,000 (60%)
Tax Savings (20%)	600,000	300,000	900,000	750,000
Net Catholic Share	2,400,000	1,200,000	3,600,000	3,000,000
Share of Others	None	1,000,000 (40%)	1,000,000	2,500,000 (40%)
Tax Savings (6%)	None	60,000	60,000	150,000
Net Share of Others	None	940,000	940,000	2,350,000
Total Catholic Share	2,400,000	1,260,000	3,660,000	3,150,000
Total Share of Others	600,000	1,240,000	1,840,000	3,100,000
			3,300,000 (Prop. Cath. share—60%)	
			360,000 (Extra burden—10.9%)	510,000 (Extra Cost—16.2%)

Population 80% Catholic

Gross Cost	$4,000,000 (4n children)	$1,250,000 (n children)	$5,250,000 (5n children)	$6,250,000 (5n children)
Catholic Share	4,000,000 (100%)	1,000,000 (80%)	5,000,000	5,000,000 (80%)
Tax Savings (20%)	800,000	200,000	1,000,000	1,000,000
Net Catholic Share	3,200,000	800,000	4,000,000	4,000,000
Share of Others	None	250,000 (20%)	250,000	1,250,000 (20%)
Tax Savings (6%)	None	15,000	15,000	75,000
Net Share of Others	None	235,000	235,000	1,175,000
Total Catholic Share	3,200,000	815,000	4,015,000	4,075,000
Total Share of Others	800,000	435,000	1,235,000	2,175,000
			4,200,000 (Prop. Cath. share—80%)	
			185,000 (Less burden—4.4%)	60,000 (Less Cost—1.5%)

Table 2—Half of the Catholic Children in Catholic Schools

	Catholic School System	Public School System	Totals of Both Systems	Single System, Public Only
Population 20% Catholic				
Gross Cost	$500,000 (½n children)	$5,625,000 (4½n children)	$6,125,000 (5n children)	$6,250,000 (5n children)
Catholics' Share	500,000 (100%)	1,125,000 (20%)	1,625,000	1,250,000 (20%)
Tax Savings (20%)	100,000	225,000	325,000	250,000
Net Catholic Share	400,000	900,000	1,300,000	1,000,000
Share of Others	None	4,500,000 (80%)	4,500,000	5,000,000 (80%)
Tax Savings (6%)	None	270,000	270,000	300,000
Net Share of Others	None	4,230,000	4,230,000	4,700,000
Total Catholic Share	400,000	1,170,000	1,570,000	1,300,000
Total Share of Others	100,000	4,455,000	4,555,000	4,950,000
			1,225,000 (Prop. Cath. share—20%)	
			345,000 (Extra burden—28.1%)	270,000 (Extra cost—20.7%)
Population 40% Catholic				
Gross Cost	$1,000,000 (n children)	$5,000,000 (4n children)	$6,000,000 (5n children)	$6,250,000 (5n children)
Catholics' Share	1,000,000 (100%)	2,000,000 (40%)	3,000,000	2,250,000 (40%)
Tax Savings (20%)	200,000	400,000	600,000	500,000
Net Catholic Share	800,000	1,600,000	2,400,000	2,000,000
Share of Others	None	3,000,000 (60%)	3,000,000	3,750,000
Tax Savings (6%)	None	180,000	180,000	225,000
Net Share of Others	None	2,820,000	2,820,000	3,525,000
Total Catholic Share	800,000	1,780,000	2,580,000	2,225,000
Total Share of Others	200,000	3,220,000	3,420,000	4,025,000
			2,400,000 (Prop. Cath. share—40%)	
			180,000 (Extra burden—7.5%)	355,000 (Extra cost—16%)

Population 60% Catholic

Gross Cost	$1,500,000 (1½n children)	$4,375,000 (3½n children)	$5,875,000 (5n children)	$6,250,000 (5n children)
Catholics' Share	1,500,000 (100%)	2,625,000 (60%)	4,125,000	3,750,000 (60%)
Tax Savings (20%)	300,000	525,000	825,000	750,000
Net Catholic Share	1,200,000	2,100,000	3,300,000	3,000,000
Share of Others	None	1,750,000 (40%)	1,750,000	2,500,000
Tax Savings (6%)	None	105,000	105,000	150,000
Net Share of Others	None	1,645,000	1,645,000	2,350,000
Total Catholic Share	1,200,000	2,205,000	3,405,000	3,150,000
Total Share of Others	300,000	2,170,000	2,470,000	3,100,000
			3,525,000 (Prop. Cath. share—60%)	
			120,000 (Less burden—3.4%)	255,000 (Extra cost—8.1%)

Population 80% Catholic

Gross Cost	$2,000,000 (2n children)	$3,750,000 (3n children)	$5,750,000 (5n children)	$6,250,000 (5n children)
Catholics' Share	2,000,000 (100%)	3,000,000 (80%)	5,000,000	5,000,000 (80%)
Tax Savings (20%)	400,000	600,000	1,000,000	1,000,000
Net Catholic Share	1,600,000	2,400,000	4,000,000	4,000,000
Share of Others	None	750,000 (20%)	750,000	1,250,000 (20%)
Tax Savings (6%)	None	45,000	45,000	75,000
Net Share of Others	None	705,000	705,000	1,175,000
Total Catholic Share	1,600,000	2,445,000	4,045,000	4,075,000
Total Share of Others	400,000	1,305,000	1,705,000	2,175,000
			4,600,000 (Prop. Cath. share—80%)	
			515,000 (Less burden—11.2%)	30,000 (Less cost—0.7%)

Explanatory Notes to Appendix C Tables

Purpose of the Tables

The purpose of these tables is to show at the highest cost the Catholic schools are likely to reach: the proportionate extra burden to Catholics of maintaining a separate school system of grade and high schools and paying taxes for the public school system, compared with the burden of ordinary citizens who support only the public school system, and the actual extra cost to Catholics of maintaining their own system and paying taxes for the public schools compared to the cost of closing their schools and placing the children in the public schools. The latter is the only basis, so far as the cost factor is concerned, for judging whether or not we should maintain a separate system.

Table 1 shows situations where all of the Catholic children attend Catholic schools.

Table 2 shows situations where only half of the Catholic children attend Catholic schools.

Assumptions

The tables are based upon the following assumptions:

1. The per pupil cost in public schools is one and one-fourth times the per pupil cost in Catholic schools. Actually at present it is about twice as much in most places. Purely for illustrative purposes, the tables assume a per pupil cost of $500 per year in the public schools, $400 in the Catholic schools.

2. The cost of the public schools is met by taxes, the burden of which falls equally upon the Catholics in the community, that is, in proportion to their numbers. The cost of the Catholic schools is borne by contributions (not by tuition) qualifying as deductions under the federal income tax law.

3. The net savings to the Catholic community through operation of the federal income tax system of supporting their schools by contributions is 20%. The basis for this assumption is explained in Interpretation 3 below and in Appendix E.

Interpretations

1. "N" stands for any given number of children of grade and high school age. The illustrations used in the tables are based on "n" equalling 2,500 children; "5n" stands for the total number of school children in a

given community, and it is used because the examples based on different population ratios are in fifths; that is, they show the situation in communities where Catholics constitute 20%, 40%, 60% and 80% of the total population and where all (Table 1), or half (Table 2), of the Catholic children are in Catholic schools. The results under any intermediate percentages can be estimated proportionately. Or they can be figured exactly by using the actual numbers and percentages in any community.

If there are any significant number of children in other religious school systems (such as Lutheran) in a community, this number may be added to those in the Catholic school system. This will lower the Extra Cost to Catholics.

Take the first example in Table 1. If there are 12,500 children of grade and high school age in Center City, and 20% of the children are Catholic, 2,500 children will be educated in the Catholic schools and 10,000 in the public schools. In this example, "n" equals 2,500; "4n" equals 10,000; and "5n" equals 12,500. Similarly, in Table 2, half of the Catholic children (1,250) are shown as "½n"; the rest go into the public school column which becomes 11,250 or "4-½n."

The cost ratio of one to one and one-fourth means that it costs 25% more per pupil to educate a child in the public schools. At the present time the ratio is one to two or more in most communities. For example, in the Milwaukee area at present, the public grade school cost is about $600 and the high school cost about $1,000. The corresponding Catholic school costs are said to be about $300 and $500.

A note of caution here: Catholic school cost figures are not as accurate as public school cost figures. There is no uniform cost accounting system and some expenses may not have been taken into account. But the one to one and one-fourth ratio used in the tables as an ultimate ratio is fairly reliable. Despite mounting expenses for reasonably competitive salaries and for an increasing number of lay teachers, the Catholic schools will always be significantly less expensive per pupil than the public schools. Less gingerbread in buildings and lower administrative costs and teacher salaries will save money. Substantial numbers of clergy and religious will continue staffing Catholic schools for lower salaries than lay teachers receive. However, school administrators will have to pay religious teachers enough money for a proper education. They will also have to pay competitive salaries to lay teachers to obtain and hold competent teachers. Salaries of religious teachers will be only what they need because the orders are not profit-making institutions and the needs of their members are likely to remain only one-fourth to one-third that of the market rates for lay teachers whose salaries must cover the needs of a family. Salaries for lay teachers may not have to be quite as much as those paid by the public schools for persons of equal ability. Present indications are that most lay teachers will accept less in the Catholic schools than in the public schools because of greater job satisfaction, apparently a composite of dedication to an apostolate and a belief that working conditions are more pleasant. However this situation may not continue indefinitely.

A characteristic pattern found today would be a community in which the average salary of public school teachers is $8,000, that of Catholic lay teachers $6,000, and that of Catholic religious teachers $1,500, with the proportion of lay teachers to religious about one to one. Curiously enough, teachers' salaries in both school systems represent about the same percentage of total operating expenses (70 to 75%) so that the ratio of per pupil operating cost between the two systems is rather accurately reflected by the ratio of teachers' average salaries between the two systems. Today, assuming that figures just mentioned are reasonably correct, this ratio is $6,000 plus $1,500 for salaries to two $8,000 salaries; or $7,500 for salaries compared to $16,000 for salaries, i.e., about 1 to 2.

Now suppose that eventually the average salary of teachers in the public schools becomes $10,000, that of lay teachers in Catholic school $10,000, that of religious teachers $2,500, and the ratio of lay to religious teachers (whether because of a severe decline in numbers of religious devoted to education at the present level of school enrollment, or partly for that reason and partly because of a much higher level of enrollment) becomes three to one. The per pupil operating cost ratio between Catholic schools and public schools would then be 3($10,000) plus $2,500 to 4($10,000), or $32,500 to $40,000, or about 1 to 1¼. It should continue to be possible to realize a capital cost differential of at least that amount.

Because of the lesser cost of building, teachers and administration, the Catholic schools will always be assured of a substantially lower per pupil cost than the public schools. The one to one and a fourth is, we believe, a safe prediction for the long run.

The great increase in absolute dollar costs is of no significance. Public school costs are increasing equally, and Catholics must pay their proportionate share of those costs. But the comparative per pupil cost of the two systems is significant. We must not lose sight of this fact.

Tax Savings

These are individual federal income tax savings based upon the assumption that the cost of running the Catholic schools is borne by contributions which are deductible. To achieve this saving, tuition (which is not tax deductible) will have to be supplanted by contributions. Appendix E explains the calculation that net savings to the Catholic community, if it supports its schools by contributions rather than by tuition, would be 20%. Even greater savings would be realized if, as suggested in Appendix E, contributions were made in accordance with ability to pay, instead of at the flat percentages Appendix F shows as the present pattern.

Again, using the first example in Table 1 and applying it to a community of 12,500 children when 2,500 are in the Catholic schools, and the public school per pupil cost is $500, the Catholic $400: the Catholic school cost of $1,000,000 is met by tax deductible contributions. Initially, federal income tax savings will be about $250,000. Other taxpayers, in effect, contribute the rest. But since Catholics themselves constitute 24% of the "others," the actual saving to the Catholics in this example is $200,000 net.

Note that tax savings appear in the public school column as well. This is because the public schools are supported wholly by taxes of one kind or another, all of which are tax deductible for federal income tax purposes. The only assumption made here is that Catholics as a group are economically as well off as the population as a whole, and hence that the 20% net saving applies across the board. If the assumed 20% should turn out to be 15% or 25%, or any other significantly different figure than 20%, the proper dollar amounts can be calculated across the board.

Similar tax savings under state income tax laws are not taken into account because many states do not have personal income taxes. In states which have such taxes, New York and Wisconsin, for example, Catholics would save an additional five or six percentage points net. Appendix D illustrates, among other things, the effect of this additional tax saving. The important point is that the potential tax savings, the seldom noticed contribution of the general public to the support of the Catholic schools, is a substantial factor, and we should adopt contributions instead of tuition as the universal way to finance Catholic schools.

In the column, "Totals of Both Systems," note that the "Extra Burden" is not "Extra Cost." "Extra Burden" is the extra amount or percentage paid by those who support religious schools and public schools—compared with the amount paid by ordinary citizens who support only public schools. Some Catholics who usually do not know the actual amount use this comparative figure to make themselves and others feel unjustly put upon. It never amounts to anything approaching double taxation, and it shrinks rapidly as the proportion of Catholics increases.

Table 1 shows that in a community of 12,500 children of whom 2,500 are in Catholic schools, the public school cost at $500 per pupil is $5,000,000. Catholic schools cost $400 per pupil totalling $1,000,000—a grand total of $6,000,000. The proportionate Catholic share would be 20% of $6,000,000 or $1,200,000. Maintaining a separate system at $1,-000,000 plus paying taxes to support the public school system at 20% of $5,000,000, or $1,000,000, totals $2,000,000. Thus the theoretical "Extra Burden" to Catholics of the two systems would be $800,000 or 66⅔%. But these figures do not take into account the possible income tax savings mentioned above. The value of qualifying for such tax savings is shown in the example. They bring the "Extra Burden" down to $640,-000—53.3%. Note how drastically it shrinks as the Catholic population ratio increases.

The "Single System, Public Only" column illustrates the difference between maintaining Catholic schools and closing them (or not establishing them) and placing all of the children in the public schools. The two figures to compare are the "Total Catholic Share" figures in the third and fourth columns. They show that by maintaining their own system Catholics will save a great amount of taxes they would otherwise be obliged to pay to support their children in the public schools. This money can support Catholic children in Catholic schools. Every tax dollar saved is available for Catholic schools.

In the Table 1 example of a community of 12,500 school children of whom 2,500 are Catholic, the total cost of the dual system would be $6,000,000. Catholics would have to pay $2,000,000 of this. But the total cost of a wholly public system would be $6,250,000, of which Catholics would have to pay $1,250,000. This represents an additional tax burden of $250,000. On the other hand, it would cost Catholics only $1,250,000 compared to the $2,000,000 cost of supporting the two school systems. This is $750,000, or 60% more. Again, this statement does not take into account possible income tax savings. These would narrow the difference to $540,000—41.5%—as shown in the table. The "Extra Cost" of educating fewer than all of Catholic children in Catholic schools is, of course, less (Table 2).

Notice again how significantly the "Extra Cost" decreases as the

Catholic population increases. At a little under 80% the cost of maintaining a separate system compared to supporting a wholly public school system balances. This is true even with all Catholic children in Catholic schools and under the most extreme narrowing of comparative per pupil cost ratios (one to one and one-fourth) we may experience in the future. In most communities we are only about halfway to either of those points. There is no cause for whimpering, much less for defeatism.

Appendix D

Illustration of Extra Burden and Extra Cost of Maintaining Catholic Schools at Present Costs

Assumptions

1. A city 30% Catholic with 10,000 grade school children of whom 3,000 are Catholic.
2. Per pupil costs: Catholic $300, public $600 (a ratio of one to two).
3. Net federal income tax savings to Catholics through contribution financing: 20%. (For explanation of this calculation, see Appendix E).
4. Net state income tax savings to Catholics through contribution method: 6%. (Applicable rate 9.2%. Catholics constitute 35% of state's taxpayers.)

Example 1. Half of the Catholic Children in Catholic Schools.

	Catholic School System	Public School System	Totals of Both Systems	Single System, Public Only
1. Gross Cost	$450,000 (1,500 @ $300)	$5,100,000 (8,500 @ $600)	$5,550,000	$6,000,000 (10,000 @ $600)
2. Gross Share of Cost to Catholics	450,000	1,530,000 (30%)	1,980,000	1,800,000 (30%)
3. Tax Savings (20% plus 6%, rounded to 25%)	112,500	382,500	495,000	450,000
4. Net Catholic Share	337,500	1,147,500	1,485,000	1,350,000
5. Gross Share of Others	None	3,570,000 (70%)	3,570,000 (70%)	4,200,000 (70%)
6. Tax Savings (6% plus 3.2%, rounded to 10%)	None	357,000	357,000	420,000
7. Net Share of Others	None	3,213,000	3,213,000	3,780,000

				1,770,000
8. Total Catholic Share (4 + 6)	337,500	1,504,500	1,842,000	
9. Total Share of Others (3 + 7)	112,500	3,595,500	3,708,000	4,230,000
			1,665,000 (Prop. Cath. share-30%)	
			177,000 (Extra Burden-10.6%)	72,000 (Extra Cost-4%)

Example 2. All of the Catholic Children in Catholic Schools.

1. Gross Cost	$900,000 (3,000 @ $300)	$4,200,000 (7,000 @ $600)	$5,100,000	$6,000,000 (10,000 @ $600)
2. Gross Share of Cost to Catholics	900,000 (30%)	1,260,000 (30%)	2,160,000 (30%)	1,800,000 (30%)
3. Tax Savings (25%)	225,000	315,000	540,000	450,000
4. Net Catholic Share	675,000	945,000	1,620,000	1,350,000
5. Gross Share of Others	None	2,940,000 (70%)	2,940,000 (70%)	4,200,000 (70%)
6. Tax Savings (10%)	None	294,000	294,000	420,000
7. Net Share of Others	None	2,646,000	2,646,000	3,780,000
8. Total Catholic Share (4 + 6)	675,000	1,239,000	1,914,000	1,770,000
9. Total Share of Others (3 + 7)	225,000	2,961,000	3,186,000	4,230,000
			1,530,000 (Prop. Cath. share-30%)	
			384,000 (Extra Burden-25.1%)	144,000 (Extra Cost-8%)

Conclusions

The extra cost of educating all Catholic children in Catholic schools in this city, as against closing the schools and placing the children in the public schools, is only $48 per pupil per year. This is an 8% premium for a quality Catholic education.

The difference in extra cost of maintaining schools for all Catholic children and maintaining schools for half of the children is about $72,000. The cost of maintaining an adequate CCD program for the 1,500 children not in Catholic schools would soak up a large part of this difference.

The great significance of financing the schools by contributions rather than by tuition is manifest.

Appendix E

Sources of Federal Individual Income Taxes for 1967

	Number of Returns	%	AGI[1] ($ millions)	%	Av. Tax	Total Tax ($ millions)	%
Totals	71,651,909		504,809		1,072	62,920	
By *class*							
Under $600	4,080,211	5.7	1,363	0.3			
$600–1,000	3,319,019	4.6	2,641	0.5	8	5	0.0 [2]
$1,000–2,000	7,561,689	10.6	11,224	2.2	75	374	0.6
$2,000–3,000	5,905,285	8.2	14,731	2.9	182	793	1.3
$3,000–4,000	5,697,243	8.0	19,917	3.9	282	1,384	2.2
$4,000–5,000	5,451,222	7.6	24,522	4.8	385	1,914	3.0
$5,000–6,000	5,186,943	7.2	28,539	5.6	489	2,430	3.9
$6,000–7,000	5,219,185	7.3	33,925	6.7	599	3,066	4.9
$7,000–8,000	5,111,630	7.1	38,272	7.6	704	3,563	5.7
$8,000–9,000	4,477,651	6.2	38,025	7.5	846	3,766	6.0
$9,000–10,000	3,839,287	5.4	36,412	7.2	936	3,775	6.0
$10,000–15,000	10,385,432	14.5	124,433	24.6	1,411	14,627	23.2
$15,000–20,000	2,761,962	3.9	46,864	9.2	2,381	6,562	10.4
$20,000–50,000	1,958,137	2.7	55,056	10.9	5,265	10,282	16.3
$50,000–100,000	260,607 ⎫		17,203	3.4	19,440	5,055	8.0
$100,000–200,000	51,352 ⎪		6,768	1.3	49,082	2,509	4.0
$200,000–500,000	12,738 ⎬ 0.5		3,651	0.7	119,111	1,505	2.4
$500,000–1,000,000	2,096 ⎪		1,410	0.3	294,087	605	1.0
$1,000,000 and over	835 ⎭		1,685	0.3	871,042	707	1.1

(1) Adjusted gross income.   (2) Less than 0.01%.

Explanatory Note

The above data was compiled from a 1969 publication of the Internal Revenue Service. Similar publications are issued annually but figures are nearly three years old. However, each publication contains comparable historical data for the previous eight or ten years. As long as the economy remains as stable as it has been since the end of the Korean War, the trends shown can fairly safely be extrapolated to reflect more up-to-date conditions. For example, the above table shows that in 1967, 51% of total adjusted gross income was enjoyed by the 21.6% of the taxpayers who received $10,000 or more. After all deductions and exemptions were taken into account, this group paid 66.4% of all individual income taxes.

In 1966, the $10,000 and over group included only 19.6% of the taxpayers who enjoyed only 46.7% of total adjusted gross income and paid only 62% of the taxes. These percentages have increased steadily. The 1969 figures will probably show that about 25% of taxpayers will be in the $10,000 and over group who enjoy nearly 60% of adjusted gross income and pay about 70% of individual income taxes.

In this group, exemptions reduce adjusted gross income by about one-eighth. This exposed them to a minimum rate of 22%, and a maximum rate of 70%. Considering the nearly 70% of taxes paid by this group, it seems safe to say that, except for contributions and other deductions, more than half of total taxes would be collected at rates ranging from 25% to 70%; less than half would be figured at rates ranging from 14% to 25%. So 25% seems to be a safe figure to pick as the average saving on contributions made by all classes of taxpayers. Perhaps some day the Internal Revenue Service will publish the exact figure. Without a breakdown of the very large $10,000 to $15,000 class, it is impossible to calculate the exact figure from published statistics.

By the same token, this would be the initial saving made by Catholics as a group where all income classes contributed to the support of the schools the same percentage of their income. On the other hand, if people in higher income brackets contributed a higher percentage of their incomes, the initial saving would be more than 25%.

In any event, initial tax savings must be netted. When a particular deduction is permitted for a particular class, such as Catholics who contribute to religious schools, the saving to them is made up by all taxpayers. Catholics constitute 24% of all taxpayers. So the net saving to Catholics as a group would be 76% of 25% or approximately 20%.

Appendix F

Average Deductions Claimed on 1966 Federal Income Tax Returns

Adjusted Gross Income	Interest	% of AGI	Taxes	% of AGI	Medical	% of AGI	Other	% of AGI	Contributions	% of AGI
$5–6,000	387	7.0	340	6.2	373	6.8	131	2.4	202	3.6
6–7,000	452	7.0	391	6.0	359	5.5	139	2.1	216	3.3
7–8,000	515	7.0	463	6.2	356	4.7	150	2.0	226	3.0
8–9,000	576	6.8	517	6.1	371	4.4	149	1.7	250	3.0
9–10,000	636	6.8	581	6.1	379	4.0	159	1.6	268	2.8
10–15,000	730	5.8	712	5.7	414	3.3	181	1.4	326	2.5
15–20,000	910	5.2	995	5.7	567	3.2	225	1.3	466	2.6
20–50,000	1,301	3.7	1,603	4.6	1,032	2.9	381	1.1	819	2.3
50–100,000	2,816	3.7	3,514	4.6	2,084	2.7	1,096	1.4	2,267	3.0
100,000 or more	9,327	*	10,221	*	2,996	*	4,471	*	14,035	*

* Impossible to average. An assumed AGI average of $300,000, however, fits the percentage trends pretty well. At this figure, the respective percentages would be 3.1, 3.4, 1.0, 1.4, and 4.6.